Henry Lytton Bulwer

Sir Robert Peel

An historical sketch

Henry Lytton Bulwer

Sir Robert Peel
An historical sketch

ISBN/EAN: 9783337012205

Printed in Europe, USA, Canada, Australia, Japan

Cover: Foto ©ninafisch / pixelio.de

More available books at **www.hansebooks.com**

SIR ROBERT PEEL.

An Historical Sketch.

BY

HENRY, LORD DALLING AND BULWER,

AUTHOR OF 'HISTORICAL CHARACTERS,' ETC.

LONDON:

RICHARD BENTLEY & SON, NEW BURLINGTON STREET,
Publishers in Ordinary to Her Majesty.
1874.

[The Right of Translation is Reserved.]

PREFATORY NOTE.

Some delay has arisen in giving to the public the latest historical sketch which occupied the thoughts of Lord Dalling. It was hoped that amongst his voluminous papers would be found his estimate of Lafayette, and his sketch of Lord Melbourne. Lord Dalling had collected material for these sketches, but, except in the case of Lord Melbourne, he had worked very little upon them, and the brief sketch of Lord Melbourne seems to be the production of a much earlier period, and scarcely worthy to be added to his 'Historical Characters.'

It may not be out of place here to remark the infinite pains which Lord Dalling took in the preparation of these sketches. He offered to the public no crude work, but one of which both conception and execution were the result of mature thought. Whole pages after being set up would be printed again and again, and he would spend a morning sometimes in giving more finish to the style of a few paragraphs. He resembled a great painter in being unwilling to part with his work, and carried it about with him from place to place, that he might be able to obey the inspiration of the moment, and add to it those felicitous touches which give such value to his labours.

GEORGE BENTLEY.

New Burlington Street.
October 21, 1874.

PREFACE.

THERE are many circumstances which render the character and life of the late Sir Robert Peel at this moment peculiarly interesting. They are a complement to the life and character of Mr. Canning, which we lately had before us. They, moreover, not only represent the intellect and genius of an individual, but of an epoch; and the types of men living at particular periods afford the best studies of history.

Homer is in this respect the great historian of his age, for all his men are types of his age: as in many respects they are of every age. Mr. Bagehot, in one of his admirable essays, has called the statesman with whom we are about to occupy ourselves "the business gentleman." We think, however, that he may more particularly be put forward as "the practical man." He opposed everything which at such a day or year was impracticable; he supported and carried through almost every great question of his day, when it became practical. He did not say that this thing or that was good before opinion was prepared for its being carried. He took it up and carried it, if it were good—when it could be carried. In opposing or supporting it he gave you practical reasons for his support or opposition.

His views, it has been said justly, were never remarkable: his abilities were always conspicuous. People of this disposition abound; but there is no one who represents it so strikingly. He is consequently the person to whom we are now constantly referring, when a conduct similar to that which he pursued is under judgment.

For all these reasons we offer no apology for a sketch in which we do not venture to affirm we shall say anything very new, but in which we hope to comprise almost everything that has been said, and is worth repeating.

SIR ROBERT PEEL.

PART I.

Family.—Birth.—Formation of Character.—Education at Harrow and Oxford.—Entry into Parliament.—Line adopted there.—Style of Speaking.—Becomes Secretary of Colonies.—Secretary for Ireland.—Language on the Catholic Question.—Returned as Member for the University of Oxford.—Resigned his post in Ireland.

SIR ROBERT PEEL.

PART I.

FROM BIRTH AND PARENTAGE TO HIS QUITTING IRELAND, WHERE HE ACTED FOR SOME TIME AS SECRETARY.

I.

THE family of the Peels belonged to the class of yeomanry, which in England, from the earliest times, was well known and reputed, forming a sort of intermediate link between the gentry and the commonalty, as the gentry formed an intermediate link between the great barons and the burghers or wealthy traders. The yeoman was proud of belonging to the yeomanry, and if you traced back the descent of a yeoman's family, you found it frequently the issue of the younger branch of some noble or gentle house. For some generations this family of Peel had at its head men of industry and energy, who were respected by their own class, and appeared to be gradually rising into another. The grandfather of the great Sir Robert inherited a small estate of about one hundred pounds a year, called Peel's Fold, which is still in the family. He received a fair education at a grammar-school, and married (1747) into a gentleman's family (Haworth, of Lower Darwen).

Beginning life as a farmer of his little property, he undertook, at the time that the cotton manufacture began to develop itself in Lancashire, the business of trader and printer.

The original practice had been to send up the fabricated article to Paris, where it was printed and sent back into this country for sale. Mr. Peel started a calico printing manufactory, first in Lancashire and afterwards in Staffordshire, and his success was the result of the conviction—that "a man could always succeed if he only put his will into the endeavour," a maxim which he often repeated in his later days, when as a stately old gentleman he walked with a long gold-headed cane, and wore the clothes fashionable for moderate people in the days of Dr. Johnson.

The first Sir Robert Peel was a third son. Enterprising and ambitious, he left his father's establishment, and became a junior partner in a manufactory carried on at Bury by a relation, Mr. Haworth, and his future father-in-law, Mr. Yates. His industry, his genius, soon gave him the lead in the management of this business, and made it prosperous. By perseverance, talent, economy, and marrying a wealthy heiress—Miss Yates, the daughter of his senior partner—he had amassed a considerable fortune at the age of forty.

He then began to turn his mind to politics, published a pamphlet on the National Debt, made the acquaintance of Mr. Pitt, and got returned to Parliament (1790) for Tamworth, where he had acquired a landed property, which the rest of his life was passed in increasing. He was a Church and King politician in that excitable time, and his firm contributed no less than ten thousand pounds in 1797 to the voluntary subscriptions for the support of the war. So wealthy and loyal a personage was readily created a baronet in 1800.

His celebrated son was born in 1788, two years before he himself entered public life, and on this son he at once fixed his hopes of giving an historical lustre to the name which he had already invested with credit and respectability.

II.

It was the age of great political passions, and of violent personal political antipathies and partialities. The early elevation of Mr. Pitt from the position of a briefless barrister to that of prime minister had given a general idea to the fathers of young men of promise and ability that their sons might become prime ministers too. The wealthy and ambitious manufacturer soon determined, then, that his boy, who was thought to give precocious proofs of talent, should become First Lord of the Treasury. He did not merely bring him up to take a distinguished part in politics, which might happen to be a high position in opposition or office, he brought him up especially for a high official position. It was to office, it was to power, that the boy who was to be the politician was taught to aspire; and as the impressions we acquire in early life settle so deeply and imperceptibly into our minds as to become akin to instincts, so politics became instinctively connected from childhood in the mind of the future statesman with office; and he got into the habit of looking at all questions in the point of view in which they are seen from an official position; a circumstance which it is necessary to remember.

To say nothing of the anecdotes which are told in his family of the early manifestations which Mr. Peel gave of more than ordinary ability, he was not less distinguished at Harrow as a student for his classical studies, than he was as a boy for the regularity of his conduct. I remember that my tutor, Mark Drury, who, some years previous to my becoming his pupil, had Peel in the same position, preserved many of his exercises; and on one occasion brought some of them down from a shelf, in order to show me with what terseness and clearness my predecessor expressed himself, both in Latin and English.

Lord Byron says: "Peel, the orator and statesman that was, or is, or is to be, was my form-fellow, and we were both at the top of our remove, in public school phrase. We were on good terms, but his brother was my intimate friend. There were always great hopes of Peel amongst us all, masters and scholars, and he has not disappointed them. As a scholar, he was greatly my superior;

as a declaimer and actor, I was reckoned at least his equal; as a schoolboy out of school, I was always in scrapes—he never." This character as a lad developed itself, without altering in after life.

At the University of Oxford the young man was the simple growth of the Harrow boy. He read hard, and took a double first-class, indicating the highest university proficiency both in classics and mathematics. But it is remarkable that he studiously avoided appearing the mere scholar: he shot, he boated, he dressed carefully, and, without affecting the man of fashion, wished evidently to be considered the man of the world.

As soon as he became of age, his father resolved to bring him into Parliament, and did so, in 1809, by purchasing a seat for him at Cashel.

III.

The great men of the Pittite day were passing away. The leading men at the moment were Grey, Liverpool, Petty, Perceval, Tierney, Whitbread, Romilly, Horner, Castlereagh, Canning: the genius of Sheridan had still its momentary flashes; and Grattan, though rarely heard, at times charmed and startled the House of Commons by his peculiar manner and original eloquence.

Brougham, Palmerston, Robinson, were Peel's contemporaries. The Duke of Portland was prime minister; Perceval, the leader of the House of Commons; Canning, minister of foreign affairs; and Lord Castlereagh, secretary of war. But this ministry almost immediately disappeared: the Duke of Portland resigning, Lord Castlereagh and Canning quarrelling, and Mr. Perceval, as prime minister, having to meet Parliament in 1810 with the disastrous expedition of Walcheren on his shoulders. Young Peel, not quite twenty-two, was chosen for seconding the address, and did so in a manner that at once drew attention towards him. He was then acting as private secretary to Lord Liverpool, who had become minister of war and the colonies. The condition of the Government was but ricketty: Lord Carnarvon carried against it a motion for inquiry into the conduct and policy of the expedition to the Scheldt; and, subsequently, it could only obtain a vote of confidence by a majority of twenty-three, which, in the days of close boroughs, was thought equivalent to a defeat. Peel spoke in two or three debates, not ill, but not marvellously well; there was, in fact, nothing remarkable in his style; and its fluency and correctness were more calculated to strike at first than on repetition. He never failed, however, being always in some degree beyond mediocrity.

In the meantime his business qualities became more and more appreciated; and it was not long before he was appointed to the under-secretaryship of the colonies.

It was no doubt a great advantage to him that the government he had joined wanted ability.

Mr. Perceval's mediocrity, indeed, was repulsive to men of comprehensive views; but, on the other hand, it was peculiarly attractive to men of narrow-minded prejudices. The dominant prejudice of this last class — always a considerable one — was at this time an anti-Catholic one; some denouncing Romanists as the pupils of the devil, others considering it sufficient to say they were the subjects of the Pope. Mr. Peel joined this party, which had amongst it some statesmen who, sharing neither the bigotry nor the folly of the subalterns in their ranks, thought, nevertheless, that it would be impossible to satisfy the Catholics in Ireland without dissatisfying the Protestants in

England, and were therefore against adding to the strength of a body which they did not expect to content.

IV.

Mr. Perceval's unexpected death was a great blow to the anti-Catholics, and appeared likely to lead to the construction of a new and more liberal Cabinet. The general feeling, indeed, was in favour of a Cabinet in which the eminent men of all parties might be combined; and a vote in favour of an address to the Regent, praying him to take such measures as were most likely to lead to the formation of a strong administration, passed the House of Commons.

But it may almost be said that eminent men are natural enemies, who can rarely be united in the same Cabinet, and are pretty sure to destroy or nullify each other when they are. The attempt at such an union was, at all events, on this occasion a signal failure.

Thus, luckily for the early advancement of Mr. Peel, Lord Liverpool had to construct a government as best he could out of his own adherents, and the under-secretary of the colonies rose at once to the important position of Secretary for Ireland, to which the Duke of Richmond, a man more remarkable for his joviality than his ability, and a strenuous anti-Catholic, was sent as Lord Lieutenant.

V.

The Catholic question was to be considered an open one in the new Cabinet, but the Irish Government, as I have shown, was altogether anti-Catholic. This was in fact the strong bias of the administration, and also of the Prince Regent, who, regardless of former promises and pledges, had now become an avowed opponent of the Catholic claims. These claims, moreover, were strongly opposed by the feelings, at that time greatly excited, of the English clergy, and, speaking generally, of the English people.

Under such circumstances, a Catholic policy was at the moment impracticable; that is, it could not be carried out: for to carry out a policy opposed by the sovereign, opposed by the premier (who had been selected because his most able opponents could not form a Cabinet), opposed by the English clergy, opposed by the general sentiment of the

English people, was impracticable, whatever might be said theoretically in its favour.

Mr. Peel, then, in taking up the anti-Catholic policy, took up the practical one.

The Catholics themselves, indeed, destroyed for a while all hope in their cause, for when the most considerable of their supporters, in order to dissipate the alarm of their co-religionists, proposed certain guarantees for maintaining the authority of the King and the State over the Catholic priesthood, although the English Catholics and the highest orders of Catholics in Ireland willingly agreed to these guarantees, the more violent of the Irish Catholics, with Mr. O'Connell at their head, joining the most violent anti-Catholics, vehemently opposed them. Moderate people were, therefore, crushed by the extremes. Even Grattan was for a moment put on one side.

This was unfortunate for Mr. Peel, who would willingly have been as moderate as his situation would permit him, but could only at such a crisis live with violent people, and thus obtained the nickname of "Orange Peel," so that after different altercations with Mr. O'Connell—altercations which nearly ended in a duel—he found himself, almost in his own despite, regarded by both

Protestants and Catholics as the great Protestant champion.

It was in this position that he made, in 1817 (on an unsuccessful motion of Mr. Grattan's), a very remarkable speech, the success of which Sir James Mackintosh attributes to its delivery.

" Peel," he says, " made a speech of little merit, but elegantly and clearly expressed, and so well delivered as to be applauded to excess. He now fills the important place of spokesman to the intolerant faction.".

The speech, however, had other merits than those Sir James acknowledged, and I quote a passage which subsequently formed the groundwork of all Mr. Peel's anti-Catholic speeches.

" If you give them " (the Catholics) " that fair proportion of national power to which their numbers, wealth, talents, and education will entitle them, can you believe that they will or can remain contented with the limits which you assign to them? Do you think that when they constitute, as they must do, not this year or next, but in the natural, and therefore certain order of things, by far the most powerful body in Ireland—the body most controlling and directing the government of it; do you think, I say, that they will view with satisfaction the state of your church or their own? Do you think that if they are constituted like other men, if they have organs, senses, affections, passions, like ourselves; if they are, as no doubt they are, sincere and zealous professors of that religious faith to which they belong; if they believe your intrusive church to have usurped the temporalities which it possesses; do you think that they will not aspire to the re-establishment of their own church in all its ancient splendour? Is it not natural that they should? If I argue from my own feelings, if I place myself in their situation, I answer that it is. May I not then, without throwing any calumnious imputations upon any Roman Catholics, without proclaiming (and grossly should I injure them if I did) such men as Lord Fingal or Lord Gormanston to be disaffected and disloyal, may I not, arguing from the motives by which men are actuated, from the feeling which nature inspires, may I not question the policy of admitting those who must have views hostile to the religious establishments of the State to the capacity of legislating for the interests of those establishments, and the power of directing the Government, of which those establishments form so essential a part?"

VI.

Have we not seen that every word I have been quoting is practically true? Are we not beginning to acknowledge the difficulty of maintaining a Protestant Church establishment in Ireland in the face of a large majority of Irish Catholic representatives? Are we not beginning to question the possibility of upholding an exclusive church belonging to a minority, without a government in which that minority dominates? Do we not now acknowledge the glaring sophistry of those who contended that the Catholics having once obtained their civil equality would submit with gratitude to religious inferiority? Mr. Peel saw and stated the case pretty clearly as it stood; the whole condition of Ireland, as between Catholic and Protestant, was involved in the question of Catholic emancipation, and as the avowed champion of Protestant ascendancy, he said, "do not resign your outworks as long as you can maintain them, if you have any serious design to keep your citadel." But the very nature of his argument showed in the clearest manner that we were ruling against the wishes and interests of the large majority of the Irish people; that we were endeavouring to maintain an artificial state of things in Ireland which was not the natural growth of Irish society;—a state of things only to be maintained by force, and which, the day that we were unable or unwilling to use that force, tumbled naturally to pieces. It is well to bear this in mind.

The anti-Catholic party, however, accepted Mr. Peel's argument; they did not pretend to say that they governed by justice; and they applauded their orator for showing that, whenever there was an attempt to govern justly, as between man and man, and not unjustly, as between Protestant and Catholic, their cause would be lost.

His reward was the one he most valued. Mr. Abbott, then Speaker, represented the University of Oxford. Mr. Abbott was made a peer, and Mr. Peel, through the interest of Lord Eldon and of the party that Sir James Mackintosh calls the intolerant one, was elected in his place, in spite of the well-known and favourite ambition of Mr. Canning.

With this result of his Irish administration Mr. Peel was satisfied. All the duties attached to his place he had regularly and punctually fulfilled.

His life had been steady and decorous in a country where steadiness and decorum were peculiarly meritorious because they were not especially demanded. In all matters where administrative talents were requisite he had displayed them: the police, still called " Peelers," were his invention. He protected all plans for education, except those which, by removing religious inequalities and animosities, and infusing peace into a discordant society, would have furnished the best; and with a reputation increasing yearly in weight and consideration, resigned his post, and escaped from a scene, the irrational and outrageous contentions of which were out of harmony with his character.

SIR ROBERT PEEL.

PART II.

Currency.—Views thereupon.—Chairman in 1859 of Finance Committee.—Conduct as to the Queen's trial.—Becomes Home Secretary.—Improvement of police, criminal law, prisons, &c.—Defends Lord Eldon, but guards himself against being thought to share his political tendencies, and declares himself in favour in Ireland of a general system of education for all religions, and denounces any attempt to mix up conversion with it.—Begins to doubt about the possibility of resisting the Catholic claims.—The Duke of York dies, and Lord Liverpool soon after follows.—Question of Premiership between the Duke of Wellington and Mr. Canning.—Peel sides with the Duke of Wellington.

SIR ROBERT PEEL.

PART II.

FROM QUELLING IRELAND TO SECEDING FROM THE GOVERNMENT OF MR. CANNING.

I.

THE great practical question at issue, on Mr. Peel's return from Ireland, was the currency.

The Bank, in 1797, declared, with the consent of the Government, that its notes would not be converted, on presentation, into gold.

At the time this was, perhaps, a necessary measure. It enabled the Bank to make large advances to the State, which it could not have made otherwise, and without which the Government would have found it difficult to maintain the struggle of life and death it was engaged in. We did, in fact, in our foreign war, what the United States lately did in their domestic war; but the commercial consequences of such a measure were inevitable.

If the Bank gave a note convertible into gold on presentation it gave gold: if it gave paper, which simply specified the obligation to pay gold for it some day or other, the value of the note depended on the credit attached to the promise. The promise to do a thing is never entirely equivalent to doing it; consequently, it was utterly impossible that a bank note, not immediately convertible into gold, could have precisely the same value as gold. Gold, therefore, would have a value of its own, and a bank-note a value of its own. Moreover, as the value of the bank-note depended on the faith placed in it, if it had been merely required for home trade, the decrease in value would have been small; because the English people had confidence in the Bank of England and in the Government which sustained it; but in all foreign transactions the case was different. If an English merchant had to purchase goods on the Continent and he sent out bank-notes, the merchant at St. Petersburg would have less confidence in the English bank-note than the Manchester merchant, and he would therefore say, "No, pay me in gold; or if you want to pay me in bank-notes, I will only take them at the value I place on them." In proportion, therefore, to the extent of purchases abroad was the natural abasement of paper money at home, and the increase in the value of gold as compared with paper. Besides, paper money, resting on credit, partook of the nature of the public funds, depending also on credit. As the one fell naturally, in a long and critical war, so the other fell from the same cause, though not in the same degree; all our dealings were thus carried on in a money which had one real value and one nominal one; and the real value depending, in a great measure, on matters beyond our control. Efforts on the part of our legislature to sustain it were useless. We forbade persons giving more for a guinea than twenty-one shillings in paper money, and we forbade persons exchanging a twenty-shilling bank-note for less than twenty shillings. We tried, in short, to prevent gold and silver getting the same price in England that they could get out of it.

The inevitable consequence was, that the precious metals, in spite of stupid prohibitions against their exportation, went to those countries in which it could obtain its real value. In this manner there was, first, the transmission of coin for the maintenance of our armies; secondly, its exportation for the purposes of our commerce; and, lastly, its escape from the laws which deteriorated its value, all operating to drain England of its gold and silver; and in proportion as they became scarcer, their comparative value with paper increased, insomuch that fifteen shillings in coin became at last equivalent to twenty shillings in paper bank-notes.

Much was said as to the over-issue of bank-notes. It may always be taken for granted that where there is an incontrovertible paper, there is an over-issue of bank-notes; because the over facility of having or making money will naturally tend to the over-advance of it. But we must remember, that a currency must be in proportion to the transactions which require it; that our trade increased almost, if not quite, in proportion to the increased issue from the Bank; that the absence of coin necessitated a large employ of paper, and that there did not appear to be that multitude of bubble schemes which are the usual concomitants of a superabundant circulation. There were, in fact, quite sufficient reasons, without attributing indiscretion to the Bank, to account for the difference between its paper and the coin it was said to represent; nor is there any possibility of keeping paper money on an equality with metallic money, except by making the one immediately exchangeable for the other.

The inequality, then, between paper money and metallic money could only be remedied by re-establishing that immediate exchange. But this was not an easy matter.

II.

For many years in England every transaction had been carried on in paper. Individuals had borrowed money in it, and had received this money in bank-notes. If they were called upon to repay it in gold, they paid twenty-five per cent. beyond the capital they had received. On the other hand, if individuals had purchased annuities, the seller, whether the Government or an individual, had to pay them twenty-five per cent. more than they had purchased.

The resumption of cash payments, therefore, could not take place without great individual hardship and great public loss. There can be no doubt, also, that paper money afforded great facilities for trade; and that the sudden withdrawal of these facilities might be felt throughout every class of the population.

Thus, although Mr. Horner brought the subject before the House of Commons with great ability in 1811, it was not till 1819, when the war had ceased, and the public mind in general had been gradually prepared for terminating a situation which could not be indefinitely prolonged, that the ministers intimated their intention to deal with it by the appointment of a select committee, of which Mr. Peel was named the chairman.

Up to this period, it is to be observed, the resumption of cash payments could not have been carried; and up to this period Mr. Peel and his father, who both voted against Mr. Horner, had opposed the resumption. But the question was probably now ripe, so to speak, for being dealt with. It was a matter, therefore, of practical consideration, and Mr. Peel re-considered it; and on the 20th of May it was curious to see the venerable Sir Robert representing the ideas of his time, and coming forward with a petition in favour of paper money; and his son, the offspring of another epoch, rising, after the father had sat down, to propose a measure by which paper money (I speak of paper money not immediately convertible into gold) was to be abolished; and avowing, as he said, "without shame and remorse," a thorough change of opinion.

His proposals compelled the Government to

repay the sums which it owed to the Bank, and compelled the Bank to resume cash payments at a date which the Bank anticipated by resuming them in 1821.

Of the necessity of these measures there can be no doubt; at the same time they were calculated, as I have said, to produce momentary discontent and distress, and already much discontent and distress existed.

There was, indeed, a dark period in our history to which I have already alluded in these biographical sketches, but Peel (luckily for him) was out of office during the greater portion of that gloomy time, and never made himself prominent in it except once, when called upon as a neighbour to defend the character of the magistrates on that day still memorable, in spite of all excuses and palliations, as the day of the "Manchester massacre." He undertook and performed his very delicate task on this occasion with tact and discretion. No one, indeed, ever spoke in a less unpopular manner on an unpopular subject. Far superior to Mr. Canning, in this respect, from that calm, steady, and considerate tone which never gives offence, and which, laying aside the orator, marks the statesman, he neither attempted to excite anger, nor ridicule, nor admiration; but left his audience under the impression that he had been performing a painful duty, in the fulfilment of which he neither expected nor sought a personal triumph.

III.

From the proceedings against the Queen, which shortly followed (the old King dying in 1820), he kept as much as possible aloof. On one occasion, it is true, he defended the legal course which the Ministry had adopted for settling the question of the Queen's guilt or innocence; but he blamed the exclusion of her Majesty's name from the litany; the refusal of a ship of war to bring her to England, and of a royal residence on British soil; in short, he separated himself distinctly from any scheme of persecution, manifesting that he would not sacrifice justice to Royal favour.

The Government at this time was so weak, having suffered, even previous to the Queen's unfortunate business, which had not strengthened it, several defeats, that Lord Liverpool saw the necessity of a reinforcement, and, faithful to the system of a double-mouthed Cabinet, took in Mr. Wynn (the representative of the Grenvilles), to speak in favour of the Catholics, and Mr. Peel (as successor to Lord Sidmouth, who gave up the Home Office, but remained in the ministry), to speak against them.

The change, nevertheless, considerably affected the administration, both as to its spirit and its capacity. The Grenvillites were liberal, intelligent men generally, as well as with respect to the Catholics, and Peel was generally liberal, though hostile to the claims of the Catholic body.

Lord Sidmouth, at the Home Office, had moreover been a barrier against all improvement. His career, one much superior to his merits, had been owing to his having all George III.'s prejudices without George III.'s acuteness. He was, therefore, George III.'s ideal of a minister, and on this account had been stuck into every ministry, during George III.'s lifetime, as a kind of "*King's send*," representing the Royal mind. Uniting with Lord Eldon against every popular concession, and supporting in a dry, disagreeable manner every unpopular measure, he was as much hated as a man can be who is despised. Peel, at all events, wished to gain the public esteem. His abilities were unquestioned. He was much looked up to by his own party, much respected by the opposing one; and, as it was known that Mr. Canning had at this time engaged himself to accept the Governor-Generalship of India, every one deemed that, if the Tories should remain in power, Peel would be Lord Liverpool's inevitable successor.

The moderate and elevated tone of his language, his indefatigable attention to business, a certain singleness and individuality which belonged to him, foreshadowed the premiership. Even the fact that his father had, undisguisedly, intended him for this position, though the idea was quizzed at Peel's entry into public life, tended eventually to predispose persons to accept it; for people become accustomed to a notion that has been put boldly and steadily before them, and it is rare that a man of energy and ability does not eventually obtain a distinction for which it is known, during a certain number of years, that he is an aspirant.

But one of those accidents which often cross the ordinary course of human life—the sudden death of Lord Castlereagh and the appointment of Mr. Canning as his successor—retained the Home Secretary in a second-rate position, over which the great and marvellous success of the new foreign secretary threw a certain comparative obscurity. He was obliged, therefore, to be satisfied with continuing to pursue a subordinate, but useful career, which might place him eventually in men's minds, side by side with his more brilliant competitor.

IV.

The subject to which he now particularly devoted himself was the most useful that he could have chosen. We had at the time he entered office a police that was notoriously inefficient; prisons, which by their discipline and condition were calculated rather to increase crime than to act as a corrective to it; and laws which rendered society more criminal than the criminals it punished. One can scarcely, in fact, believe that such men as Lord Eldon and Lord Ellenborough did not think it safe to abolish the punishment of death in the case of privately stealing six shillings in a shop; and it is with a shudder that one reads of fourteen persons being hanged in London in one week in 1820, and of thirty-three executions in the year 1822.

No one reflected whether the punishment was proportionate to the offence; no one considered that the alleged criminal himself was a member of the community, and had as much right to be justly dealt with and protected against wrong as the community itself. Satisfied with the last resort of hanging, the state neglected to take suitable precautions against the committal of those acts which led to hanging; nor did it seem a matter of moment to make places of confinement places of reformation, as well as places of atonement. To Bentham, Romilly, Mackintosh, Basil Montagu, and others, we owed that improvement in the public mind which led finally to an improvement in our laws. Mr. Peel had marked and felt this gradual change of opinion; and almost immediately after he became invested with the functions of the Home Department, he promised to give his most earnest attention to the state of the police, the prisons, and the penal laws; a promise that, in the four or five succeeding years, he honourably fulfilled; thus giving to philanthropic ideas that practical sanction with men of the world, which theories acquire by being taken up by men in power.

It is true that the country was, as I have

observed, becoming desirous for the changes that Mr. Peel introduced, and that he never advocated them until, owing to the efforts of others, they had won their way with the good and the thoughtful; but it is likewise true that, so soon as they became practically possible, he took them up with zeal, and carried them against a considerable and, as it was then deemed, respectable opposition, which held fœtid dungeons, decrepid watchmen, and a well-fed gallows to be essential appendages to the British constitution.

During this time also he supported, though not conspicuously, the liberal foreign policy of Mr. Canning, and the liberal commercial policy of Mr. Huskisson. He kept, nevertheless, at the head of his own section in the Ministry, as well by his consistent opposition to the Catholic claims as by his defence of Lord Eldon, whose slowness in the administration of justice and obstinate adherence to antiquated doctrines were frequently the subject of attack. This remarkable man, one of the many emanations of the Johnsonian mind which contrived to make the most narrow-minded prejudices palatable to the most comprehensive intellect, exercised great influence over the King, over the older peers and members of the House of Commons, and over that large mass of uncertains that rallies round a man who entertains no scruples and no doubts. Mr. Peel took care, however, not to pass for a mere follower of Lord Eldon, nor a mere bigot of the ultra-Protestant party. In defending and lauding the great judge and lawyer, he said expressly : " The House will remember I have nothing to do on this occasion with the political character of the Lord Chancellor :" and again, in discussing the question of proselytism and education, he not only ridiculed the idea that some extravagant people entertained of making Catholic Ireland Protestant, but stated in so many words, " that he was for educating Catholics and Protestants together under one common system, from which proselytism should be honestly and studiously excluded." His conduct on this occasion merited particular attention. The great difficulty which he foresaw in passing Catholic emancipation was the hostile feeling between Catholics and Protestants. If that feeling were removed, and a common education secured—the best mode of modifying or removing it—the practical and political objections to Catholic emancipation ceased.

V.

The fact is that even as early as 1821, when he answered a speech from Mr. Plunkett, which he once told me was the finest he ever heard, Mr. Peel felt that the ground on which he had hitherto stood was shifting from under him; that just as it had been impracticable to carry what was called "Catholic emancipation" when he entered public life, so it was becoming more and more impracticable to resist its being carried as time advanced.

Such an impression naturally became stronger and stronger as he saw distinguished converts, from Mr. Wellesley Pole, in 1812, down to Mr. Brownlow, in 1825, going over to his opponents, whereas not a single convert was made to the views he advocated. He might still think that the hope of those who imagined that the Irish Catholics, once admitted to Parliament, would rest satisfied with that triumph, was chimerical: he might still think that the Irish Catholics would, as a matter of course, insist upon equality in all respects with the Protestants: he might still foresee that this equality, the Catholics being the majority, would lead to superiority over the Protestants: he might still believe that the Protestants, accustomed to domination, and supported by property and rank, would not submit tranquilly to numbers: he might contemplate the impossibility of maintaining a Protestant Church establishment, absorbing all the revenue accorded to religious purposes, with a Catholic representation which would feel galled and humiliated by such a preference; and he might also recognise the probability that the English Protestant clergy would take part with the Irish Protestant clergy, and denounce as an atrocious robbery what might be demanded as a simple act of justice: and yet, retaining all his former convictions against the measure he was called upon to agree to, he might feel that prolonged opposition would only serve to protract a useless struggle, and be more likely to increase the evils he foresaw than to prevent them. Such a consideration could not but deeply affect his mind, and breathe over his conduct an air of hesitation and doubt.

It is not surprising, therefore, that any one who reviews his conduct attentively during the five or six years that preceded Lord Liverpool's retirement should find evident traces of this state of thought. On one occasion he says: " No result of this debate can give me unqualified satisfaction." On another: "If I were perfectly satisfied that concession would lead to perfect peace and harmony, if I thought it would put an end to animosities, the existence of which all must lament, I would not oppose the measure on a *mere theory* of the constitution." Just previous to the Duke of York's celebrated declaration, that "whatever might be his situation in life, so help him God he should oppose the grant of political power to Roman Catholics," Peel says, on the third reading of the Catholic Relief Bill, which had been carried in the House of Commons by a majority of twenty-one, that he should record, perhaps for the last time, his vote against the concessions that it granted.

This phrase, "*for the last time*," much commented on at the time, might have alluded to the possibility of the measure then under discussion being carried; and it was generally believed that Mr. Peel meditated at this time quitting office, and even Parliament, in order not to prevent Lord Liverpool from dealing with a matter on which his own opinions differed from those to which he thought it likely that the Government would have to listen.

When, however, after the death of the Duke of

York, and the illness of Lord Liverpool, the question was whether he should desert or hold fast to a cause which had lost its most powerful supporters; whether he should abandon those with whom he had hitherto acted at the moment when victory seemed almost certain to crown their opponents, or still range himself under their banner, there was hardly a choice for an honourable man, and he spoke as follows :

"The influence of some great names has been recently lost to the cause which I support, but I have never adopted my opinions either from deference to high station, or that which might more fairly be expected to impress me—high ability. Keen as the feelings of regret must be with which the loss of those associates in feeling is recollected, it is still a matter of consolation to me that I have now the opportunity of showing my attachment to those tenets which I formerly espoused, and of showing that if my opinions are unpopular I stand by them still, when the influence and authority which might have given them currency is gone, and when I believe it is impossible that in the mind of any human being I can be suspected of pursuing my principles with any view to favour or personal aggrandizement."

VI.

This speech had a double bearing. It said, as clearly as possible, that the Catholic disabilities could not be maintained; but that the speaker could not separate himself from those with whom he had hitherto acted in opposing their removal.

The struggle was, in fact, then commencing between the Duke of Wellington, backed by Lord Eldon on the one side, and Mr. Canning, backed by the opponents of Lord Eldon on the other. The ground taken for this struggle was the Catholic question; but I doubt whether it could have been avoided if there had not been a Catholic question.

Mr. Canning had, especially of late, adopted a tone and manner of superiority which Mr. Peel and Lord Eldon chafed at, and which the Duke of Wellington could no longer brook. The constant interposition of Lord Liverpool, who, by flattering alternately the great warrior and the great orator, prevented an outbreak from either, had kept up apparent harmony. But Lord Liverpool withdrawn, it was felt, both by the Duke of Wellington and Mr. Canning, that the one or the other must be master. As to Mr. Peel he naturally saw that under Mr. Canning, both being in the House of Commons, he would be comparatively insignificant, whereas, as first lieutenant of the Duke of Wellington, the duke being in the House of Lords, he was a person of considerable importance.

The determination of the Duke of Wellington not to serve under Mr. Canning, and of Mr. Canning not to serve under the Duke of Wellington, left no alternative but to act with one or the other.

Mr. Peel has been attacked for siding with the Duke of Wellington. But was it to be expected that he should leave that section of the Ministry where he was a chief to join another where he would be a subordinate? What part could he play amidst Mr. Canning and his friends, joined by a certain portion of the Whigs with whom he was a perfect stranger? and for what public object was he called upon to make this private sacrifice?

The settlement of the great question which agitated the Empire? No; that was to be left in its actual state. The point at issue was not whether an united Cabinet should be formed to settle the Catholic question; but whether a mixed Cabinet should be formed, with the Duke of Wellington or Mr. Canning at its head, leaving the Catholic question unsettled. Let us suppose that some progress towards the settlement of this question would have been made by the choice of Mr. Canning

— which is doubtful — this was a progress that would rather have kept up agitation and not have stilled it.

There is, indeed, an immense difference between concurring with people with whom you have previously been acting in order to terminate an affair, and an alliance which does not terminate the affair, with persons whom you have previously been opposing. It would, I think, have been easier for Mr. Peel to join Mr. Canning in an attempt to form a Cabinet which should bring forward a Catholic Relief Bill, than to join him in forming a Cabinet on the same principles as those on which the Duke of Wellington would have formed one.

I know that I do not give to these transactions the precise colour given to them by Mr. Peel himself, and that he says, in a letter of the 19th April to Lord Eldon, that if he had thought as Mr. Canning did on the Catholic question, or if Mr. Canning had thought as he did, he would have served under Mr. Canning; but this is creating an imaginary case in order to put a particular interpretation on a real one.

I believe, notwithstanding the pains taken to make a personal question appear a public one, that the dispute as to the premiership was in reality a personal one; but at the same time based on motives which if personal were not dishonourable. At all events, Mr. Canning deemed Mr. Peel's conduct under all circumstances so natural that he was neither surprised nor offended by it. Their partisans, as it always in such cases happens, were bitter; and Mr. Peel has been much blamed for the violence of his brother-in-law, Mr. Dawson. Every one, however, knows the proverb, "Save me from my friends, and I will save myself from my enemies!" and I have little doubt that so profound an axiom originated in the wisdom of an experienced statesman. But Mr. Pitt had not been able to temper Mr. Canning's criticisms against Mr. Addington, and Mr. Peel would have found it a still harder task to moderate the anger of his *protégés* against Mr. Canning.

It is useless dwelling longer on this epoch. Mr. Canning came into power at the head of a Government composed of heterogeneous materials, and closed his brilliant life without any solid advantages having attended his momentary triumph. The attempt to continue his administration without him was like that which had previously been made to continue Mr. Fox's ministry after the death of that great statesman. In both cases the Government was the man.

SIR ROBERT PEEL.

PART III.

Fall of the Goderich ministry.—Formation of the Cabinet under the Duke of Wellington.—Policy of that Cabinet.—Its junction with Mr. Canning's friends.—The secession of these, and the defeat of Mr. Fitzgerald in the Clare election.—Majority in the House of Commons in favour of Catholic claims.—The language of the House of Lords.—The conviction now brought about in the mind of Mr. Peel, that there was less danger in settling the Catholic claims than in leaving them unsettled.—The effect produced by this conviction on the administration.—The propositions brought forward in consequence in Parliament.—Carrying of these propositions through the two Houses.—Sir Robert Peel's conduct and sentiments throughout the discussion of the measure he had advocated.

SIR ROBERT PEEL

Part III.

FROM THE GODERICH MINISTRY TO THE CARRYING OF THE CATHOLIC QUESTION.

I.

LORD GODERICH soon perished as premier because, though a clever and accomplished man in a secondary place, he had not the indescribable something which fits a man for a superior one: that which Mr. Peel might fairly have anticipated, even had Mr. Canning lived, took place. The section of the Tory party to which he belonged was recalled to office. It is evident from the private correspondence which has since been published that two plans were then discussed. One of these was to form an administration, including Lord Eldon, and excluding any but those who had declared against Mr. Canning; the other was for an administration which, excluding Lord Eldon, should comprise as many of Mr. Canning's partisans as would accept office. It is, moreover, clear that Mr. Peel not only concurred in, but recommended the latter course, notwithstanding the connection which had hitherto existed between him and the Chancellor, a man whom it would be difficult to comprehend if one did not remember that he was born under the sceptre of Johnson, whose genius generated a class of men with minds like his own, exhibiting the compatibility of the strongest prejudices with an excellent understanding. Such a man is not to be spoken of with contempt. He represented with force the epoch to which he belonged, but that epoch was worn out. Loyalty to the House of Hanover and fidelity to the Protestant Constitution had ceased to be the war cries of the day; and even that spirit of firmness, energy, and consistency, which characterised a large part of George III.'s reign, were beginning to be replaced by a tone partly of indifference, partly of moderation, partly of liberality, that to Lord Eldon was treachery and weakness. He was, therefore, left out of the new Cabinet.

On the other hand, Mr. Lamb, Mr. Huskisson, Lord Dudley, Palmerston, the Grants, were sought as associates. "What," says Mr. Peel, " must have been the fate of a Government composed of Goulburn, Sir J. Beckett, Wetherall, and myself? .... We could not have stood creditably a fortnight." Again: "I care not for the dissatisfaction of ultra-Tories."

The Duke of Wellington, in recounting his interview with the King, when the offer to form an administration was made to him, said: "The Catholic question was not to be a Cabinet question; there was to be a Protestant Lord Lieutenant, a Protestant* Lord Chancellor, and a Protestant Chancellor in Ireland." The Irish Government, however, with Lord Anglesea as Lord Lieutenant, and Mr. Stanley as Secretary, was neither in spirit nor in letter according to this programme; and the change was attributable to Mr. Peel.

This was one of his most prosperous moments. His career had gone on up to this time, gradually collecting round it those materials out of which the character of a leading statesman is formed. There was a quiet, firm regularity in the course he had followed that had not won for him the cheers that wait on brilliant success, but had secured for him a constant murmur of continued

* Protestant here is, of course, meant to signify anti-Catholic.

approbation. He had never disappointed; whatever had been expected from him he had always done. His devotion to public affairs was unremitting and unaffected; they furnished not only his sole employment, but constituted his sole amusement; his execution of the law, where he had to see to its administration, was thoroughly upright and impartial. The changes which had taken place in his opinions were towards a more liberal and, as it was then beginning to be thought, a more practical policy in commerce, a sounder system of banking, a milder code of penal legislation.

These changes had taken place in such a manner that they seemed natural, and the result of a mind that did not submit itself to any bias but that of reason. He had no longer to contend against his brilliant and lamented rival; he was no longer burthened by a patron who had been useful but had become inconvenient and out of date. He was universally looked upon as a man of liberal tendencies, one subject alone excepted. On that subject he shewed obstinacy or firmness, but not bigotry. Would he now deal with it? Could he? Was it possible, with the King and the Duke of Wellington against the Catholics, to satisfy their hopes? Or was it possible, with a House of Commons almost equally divided, to adopt such measures as would crush their expectations?

II.

There are situations which impose a policy on ministers who wish to remain ministers—this was one. It was now necessary to "mark time," if I may use a military figure of speech, making as little dust as possible. Mr. Peel tried to do so; dropping the Act against the Catholic Association, which had been found wholly inefficient, and endeavouring not to provoke agitation, though he could not quiet it.

In the meantime, the tendency of opinion against religious disqualifications manifested itself on a motion of Lord John Russell, introduced in a speech of remarkable power and ability, for removing the Test and Corporation Acts. Mr. Peel had stated with emphasis, during the administration of Mr. Canning, that he would always oppose the repeal of these Acts, and he now did oppose it; but evidently with the feeling that his opposition, which was weak, would be ineffectual. A majority, indeed, of forty-four in the House of

E

Commons declared against him; and the Government then took up the measure and carried it through both Houses. Mr. Peel, in his memoirs, gives as his reason for this course, that if he had gone out of office he would have caused great embarrassment in the conduct of affairs in general, and not altered the disposition of Parliament as to the particular question at issue; and that if he remained in office he was obliged to place himself in conformity with the feeling of the House of Commons. Almost immediately afterwards, that House pledged itself, by a majority of six, to take the state of Ireland into consideration; and, though this majority was overruled by an adverse one in the House of Lords, the language of the Duke of Wellington and of Lord Lyndhurst, who both admitted that things could not remain as they were, left little doubt that a decided system of repression or concession was about to be attempted, and that the latter system was the more likely one.

III.

Two events had occurred between the vote in the House of Commons in favour of the resolution respecting the Catholics, and the vote in the House of Lords against it, which events had, no doubt, exercised great influence on the debate in the latter assembly. First, Mr. Canning's friends had somewhat abruptly quitted the Government under the following circumstances:

East Retford had been disfranchised for corrupt practices. The question was, what should be done with the two seats for that borough? All the other members of the Government voted for leaving the seats to the district in which East Retford was situated.

Mr. Huskisson alone gave his vote for transferring the right of election to Birmingham; and on the very night of this vote (May 20, 1828) tendered his resignation, which the Duke of Wellington accepted. When the other members of the Canning party heard of Mr. Huskisson's hasty resignation, provoked, as he said, by the cross looks of some of his colleagues on the Treasury Bench, they remonstrated with him on his conduct, which rendered theirs very difficult, since they had not voted as he had done. Mr. Huskisson tried to explain and retract his resignation. But the Premier had a particular dislike to Mr. Huskisson, who had shown too much desire for office, and gave himself too many airs after getting it. He would not accept Mr. Huskisson's excuses or explanations; and his manner was thought altogether so unfriendly and overbearing that Mr. Lamb, Mr. Charles Grant, Lord Palmerston, and Lord Dudley quitted the Government with Mr. Huskisson. The second event to which I have alluded was the consequence of the first.

IV.

The secession of the Canningites had rendered it necessary to fill their places. Mr. Vesey Fitzgerald was selected to fill the place at the Board of Trade vacated by Mr. Grant. This rendered necessary a new election for Clare.

No axiom can be more true than that if you do not mean to have a door forced open you should not allow the wedge to be inserted. It is difficult to understand how George III. could permit the measure in 1793 which made Catholics electors, whilst he resolved never to grant Catholics the right to be elected. At first the Catholic voters merely chose Protestants, who promised to extend Catholic privileges when they could do this without great injury to their own interests.

Mr. O'Connell determined on straining the power of Catholic votes to the utmost. He first tried it in 1826, in Waterford, by combining an opposition against the Protestant family of the Beresfords, who had hitherto, from their large possessions, been all-powerful in the county. But property availed nothing. The word was given, and almost every tenant voted against his landlord. The Beresfords were ignominiously defeated. The next trial was a more audacious one.

There was nothing in law to prevent a Catholic from being elected to serve in Parliament; it was only on taking his seat in Parliament that he was stopped by the parliamentary oath. Of all Protestants in Ireland none were more popular, or had been more consistently favourable to the Catholic cause, than Mr. Fitzgerald. His name, his fortune, his principles, gave him every claim on an Irish Catholic constituency that a Protestant could have. He felt himself so sure of being confirmed in the seat he occupied that he prepared to meet his constituents without the slightest fear of opposition.

But it was determined that a Catholic should be his opponent; and, in order to prevent all doubt or hesitation amongst his followers, the great agitator took the field himself. He was successful; and after Mr. Fitzgerald's defeat it was to be expected that a similar defeat awaited sooner or later every other Protestant. This was a serious state of things.

The Government was much weakened by the loss of the able men who had left it, and at the same time the dangers that menaced it were greater than they had ever been before.

Lord Anglesea, who was then, as I have stated, the Irish Viceroy, a gallant soldier and a man whose judgment was good, though his language was indiscreet, declared loudly that there was no way of dealing with the Catholic organization but by satisfying the Catholics.

The considerations which these various circumstances inspired decided the mind, which as I have shown had been long wavering, of Mr. Peel; and avowing it was no longer possible to resist the Catholic claims, he thus speaks of his conduct at this juncture:

"In the interval between the discussion (he speaks of the interval between the discussion in the Lower and Upper Houses of Parliament) I had personal communication with the Duke of Wellington; I expressed great reluctance to withdraw from him such aid as I could lend him in the carrying on of the Government, particularly after the recent schism; but I reminded him that the reasons which had induced me to contemplate retirement from office in 1825 were still more powerful in 1828, from the lapse of time, from the increasing difficulties in administering the government in Ireland, and from the more prominent situation which I held in the House of Commons.

"I told him that, being in a minority in the House of Commons on the question that of all others most deeply affected the condition and prospects of Ireland, I could not, with any satisfaction to my own feelings or advantage to the public interests, perform the double functions of leading the House of Commons and presiding over the Home Department; that at an early period, therefore, my retirement must take place. I expressed at the same time an earnest hope that in the approaching discussion in the Lords, the Duke of Wellington might deem it consistent with his sense of duty to take a course in debate which should not preclude him, who was less deeply committed on the question than myself, from taking the whole state of Ireland into consideration during the recess, with the view of adjusting the Catholic question."

After the prorogation of Parliament, the course to be adopted was maturely considered.

Sir Robert Peel's opinion was already made up. He argued thus:

"The time for half measures and mixed cabinets is gone by. We must yield or resist. Can we resist? Is it practicable? I don't mean so as to keep things for a short time as they are. Can we resist effectually by at once putting down the disturbers of the public peace, who connect themselves with the Catholic cause? Can we get a ministry divided on the Catholic question to put down efficiently an agitation in favour of that question?

"If we go to a Parliament in which there is a majority in favour of the Catholic claims, and ask for its support for the purpose of coercion, will it not say it is cheaper to conciliate than coerce?

"It is of no use to consider what it would

be best to do if it were possible. Coercion is impossible.

"Well, then, we must concede what we can no longer refuse.

His letters to the Duke of Wellington, given in his memoirs, speak clearly in this sense:

"I have uniformly opposed what is called Catholic Emancipation, and have rested my opinion on broad and uncompromising grounds. I wish I could say that my views were materially changed, and that I now believed that full concessions could be made either exempt from the dangers I have apprehended from them, or productive of the full advantages which their advocates anticipate from the grant of them.

"But whatever may be my opinion upon these points, I cannot deny that the state of Ireland, under existing circumstances, is most unsatisfactory; that it becomes necessary to make your choice between different kinds and different degrees of evil—to compare the actual danger resulting from the union and organization of the Roman Catholic body, and the incessant agitation in Ireland, with prospective and apprehended dangers to the constitution or religion of the country; and maturely to consider whether it may not be better to encounter every eventual risk of concession than to submit to the certain continuance, or rather, perhaps, the certain aggravation of existing evils."*

"I have proved to you, I hope, that no false delicacy, no fear of the imputation of inconsistency, will prevent me from taking that part which present dangers and a new position of affairs may require. I am ready at any sacrifice to maintain the opinion which I now deliberately give, that there is upon the whole less of evil in making a decided effort to settle the Catholic question, than in leaving it as it has been left—an open question.

"Whenever it is once determined that an attempt should be made by the Government to settle the Catholic question, there can be, I think, but one opinion—the settlement should, if possible, be a complete one."†

The Duke of Wellington and Lord Lyndhurst, without difficulty, adopted these views. The rest of the Cabinet accepted them.

Sir Robert, however, whilst expressing himself thus clearly as to the necessity of dealing without

---

* Letter to the Duke of Wellington, August 11, 1828.
† Mr. Peel's Memorandum for the Duke of Wellington, August 25, 1828.

delay with the Catholic question, and offering, in the most unequivocal way, his personal support to the Government in doing so, desired to retire from the Administration, and it was at first settled he should do so, but finally, at the Duke of Wellington's particular and earnest solicitation, he remained.

The King's speech at the opening of Parliament spoke of the necessity of putting down the Catholic Association, and of reviewing the laws which imposed disabilities on his Majesty's Roman Catholic subjects. The authority of the Government was to be vindicated, the constitution was to be amended. Mr. Peel did not say he had altered his opinions: he did not deny the possibility of future dangers from the changes which the Government meant to propose; but he added that those distant dangers had become in his opinion less pressing and less in themselves than the dangers which, under present circumstances, would result from leaving matters as they were.

He takes as his defence upon the charge of inconsistency "the right, the duty, of a public man to act according to circumstances;" this defence is the simple, and almost the only one he uses throughout the various discussions now commencing. To

Mr. Bankes, on one occasion, he replies pertinently by an extract from a former speech made by that gentleman himself:

"Mr. Bankes hoped it would never be a point of honour with any Government to persevere in measures after they were convinced of their impropriety. Political expediency was not at all times the same. What at one time might be considered consistent with sound policy, might at another be completely impolitic. Thus it was with respect to the Roman Catholics."

On another occasion he quotes that beautiful passage from Cicero, which was the Roman orator's vindication of his own conduct:

"Hæc didici, hæc vidi, hæc scripta legi, hæc sapientissimis et clarissimis viris, et in hâc republicâ et in aliis curtatibus, monumenta nobis, literæ prodiderunt, non semper easdem sententias ab iisdem, sed, quascumque reipublicæ status, inclinatio temporum, ratio concordiæ postularent, esse defendas."

It had been arranged that a bill for suppressing the Catholic Association should be passed, before the bill for removing Catholic disabilities should be brought forward.

On the 5th of March, the Catholic Association

Bill passed the House of Lords, and on the same day the Catholic Disabilities Bill was introduced into the House of Commons—admitting Catholics to Parliament, and to the highest military and civil offices, save those connected with church patronage and with the administration of the Ecclesiastical law, on taking an oath described in the Act; and Mr. Peel, in opening the debate, repeats with earnestness and solemnity his previous declaration:

" On my honour and conscience, I believe that the time is come when less danger is to be apprehended to the general interests of the Empire, and to the spiritual and temporal welfare of the Protestant establishment in attempts to adjust the Catholic question than in allowing it to remain in its present state. I have already stated that such was my deliberate opinion; such the conclusion to which I felt myself forced to come by the irresistible force of circumstances; and I will adhere to it: ay, and I will act on it, unchanged by the scurrility of abuse, by the expression of opposite opinions, however vehement or general; unchanged by the deprivation of political confidence, or by the heavier sacrifice of private friendships and affections."

He shows the difficulties that had existed since the time of Mr. Pitt, in forming a cabinet united in its views with respect to the Catholics; the state of things that experience had proved to be the consequence of a divided one; the final necessity of some decided course. The authority which those who were hostile to English rule had acquired, and were acquiring amidst the distracted councils of the English Government; the power already granted by previous concessions; and the dangers which could not but follow the exercise of this power for the purpose of counteracting the law, or procuring a change in it.

It had been argued that the elective franchise already gave parliamentary influence to the Catholics. In reply to this it had been suggested that we could withdraw that source of influence. "No; we cannot," replies Mr. Peel, with some eloquence, "replace the Roman Catholics in the condition in which we found them, when the system of relaxation and indulgence began. We have given them the means of acquiring education, wealth, and power. We have removed with our own hands the seal from a vessel in which a mighty spirit was inclosed; but it will not, like the Genius in the fable, return to its narrow confines and enable us to cast it back to the obscurity from which we evoked it."

He does not say who is to blame for the state of things he thus describes. He does not seem to care. He describes a situation which it is necessary to deal with, and never stopping to burthen the argument with his own faults or merits, thus continues:

"Perhaps I am not so sanguine as others in my expectations of the future; but I have not the slightest hesitation in saying that I fully believe that the adjustment of this question in the manner proposed will give better and stronger securities to the Protestant interest and the Protestant establishment than any that the present state of things admits of, and will avert dangers *impending and immediate*. What motive, I ask, can I have for the expression of these opinions but an honest conviction of their truth?"

It was this general impression that he was honest, and that he was making great personal sacrifices, which, no doubt, rendered his task easier; and when, after opening the way to a new election by the resignation of his seat, he was defeated in a contest for the University of Oxford, the eulogy of Sir James Graham spoke the public sentiment:

"I cannot boast of any acquaintance with that

right honourable gentleman (Mr. Peel) in private life. I have been opposed to him on almost all occasions since I entered into public life. I have not voted with him on five occasions, I believe, since I entered into Parliament. I think him, however, a really honest and conscientious man; and considering the sacrifices which he has recently made—the connections from which he has torn himself—the public attachments which he has broke asunder—the dangers which he might have created by an opposite course — the difficulties which he might have created by adhering to an opposite system — the civil war which he has avoided by departing from it,—and the great service which he has rendered to the State by the manly avowal of a change of opinion:—considering all these circumstances, I think the right honourable gentleman entitled to the highest praise, and to the honest respect of every friend of the Catholics."

One hostile feeling, however, still rankled in the heart of the Liberal ranks;—the party whose opposition had wearied out the generous and excitable spirit of Mr. Canning, was about to enjoy the triumph of Mr. Canning's opinions.

The dart, envenomed with this accusation, had

more than once been directed at Mr. Peel's reputation. He felt it necessary to show that it made a wound which he did not consider that he deserved. He had been praised by many for having settled the long-pending differences which his propositions were to compose.

In answering Sir Charles Wetherell, he says: " The credit of settling this question belongs to others, not to me. It belongs, in spite of my opposition, to Mr. Fox, to Mr. Grattan, to Mr. Plunkett, to the gentlemen opposite, and to an illustrious and Right Honourable friend of mine who is now no more. I will not conceal from the House that, in the course of this debate, allusions have been made to the memory of that Right Honourable friend, which have been most painful to my feelings. An honourable baronet has spoken of the cruel manner in which my Right Honourable friend was hunted down. Whether the honourable baronet was one of those who hunted him down I know not. But this I do know—that whoever joined in an inhuman cry against my Right Honourable friend, I did not. I was on terms of the most friendly intimacy with him up to the very day of his death; and I say, with as much sincerity as the heart of man can speak, that

F

I wish he was now alive to reap the harvest which he sowed."

It was a consummate touch of art on the part of the orator thus to place himself in the position of the conquered, when others proclaimed him the conqueror; in this way smothering envy, and quieting reproach.

The Bill passed through the House of Commons on the 30th of March, by a majority of 320 to 142; and was carried in the House of Lords on the 10th of April, 1829, by a majority of 213 to 109. On the 19th of April this great measure received the Royal assent.

It is useless to protract the narrative of this memorable period; but I will not close it without observing that there was one still living to whom the end of the battle, which had begun so long ago, was as glorious and as gratifying as it could have been to the illustrious statesman who was no more. Justifying, more, perhaps, than any statesman recorded in our annals, the classical description of the just and firm man, Lord Grey had, through a long series of disappointing years —with an unaffected scorn for the frowns of the monarch, and the shouts of the mob—proclaimed the principles of civil equality of which his bitterest opponents were at last tardily willing to admit the necessity.

> " Justum et tenacem propositi virum
> Non civium ardor prava jubentium,
> Non vultus instantis tyranni
> Mente quatit solidâ."

But the feelings of the great peer were in bitter contrast with those of the humiliated sovereign.

The change of George IV. from the friend to the enemy of the Catholic cause had been sudden; up to the formation of the Liverpool ministry, he was supposed to be favourable to it—ever afterwards he was most hostile. It is not to be supposed that he had not understood at an early period of life the value of the coronation oath, and all that in the later period of his life he drivelled over, as to the Protestant Constitution and the Protestant Succession. But the fact is, that the haughty bearing of Lord Grey, during those various questions which arose as to the formation of a new Government, shortly after the Regency, had deeply wounded and irritated the Regent. Out of his animosity to Lord Grey had grown up his animosity to the Catholics. The politician and his policy were mixed up together in the royal mind. He had kept the politician out of his cabinet; but that politician's policy now stormed it.

The mortification was severe.

From the summer of 1828, till the beginning of 1829, it was impossible to get from his Majesty a clear adoption of the principle that the Government should treat the Catholic question with the same freedom as any other. When this was granted, another battle was fought over the opening speech, and finally, on the 3rd of March, when the great ministerial propositions were to be brought before Parliament, he refused his assent to them, and the Wellington ministry was for some hours out of office.

The struggle continued throughout the Parliamentary discussions, the King's aversion to Mr. Peel became uncontrollable, and he did not attempt to disguise it.

But the leader of the House of Commons bore the sulky looks of the Sovereign with as much composure—a composure that was by no means indifference—as he bore the scurrility of the press, and the taunts of the Tory Opposition.

The conviction that he was acting rightly in a great cause made him a great man: and he faced the storm of abuse that assailed him with a proud complacency.

SIR ROBERT PEEL.

PART IV.

Mr. O'Connell's opposition in Ireland.—The general difficulties of the Government.—The policy it tried to pursue.—Its increasing unpopularity.—Its policy towards Don Miguel.—William IV.'s accession.—The Revolution in Paris.—The cry now raised in England for Reform.—The King's opening Speech on convocation of new Parliament.—The discontent against the Government it excited.—The Duke of Wellington opposed to any change in the Constitution.—Postponement of Lord Mayor's dinner to the new Sovereign.—Impressions this created.—The Duke's administration in a minority in the House of Commons.—His resignation.—Earl Grey's appointment as Premier.—Personal description of Sir Robert Peel at this time.—The Reform Bill.—Sir Robert Peel's conduct thereon.—Its success in the country.—The large majority returned by new elections in favour of it.—Its opposition in the House of Lords.—Lord Grey's resignation and resumption of office.—The passing of his Reform Bill through both Houses.

SIR ROBERT PEEL.

PART IV.

FROM THE PASSING OF THE CATHOLIC RELIEF BILL TO THE PASSING OF THE REFORM BILL.

I.

I HAVE said that Sir Robert Peel was proud of having made great sacrifices for a great cause. There can be little doubt that he had prevented a civil war in which many of the most eminent statesmen in England and all the eminent statesmen of foreign countries would have considered that the Irish Catholics were in the right. At the same time he did not derive from the course he had taken the hope which many entertained that all Irish feuds would henceforth cease, and that it would become easy to establish in Ireland the satisfaction and tranquillity that were found in other parts of our empire. He did, however, deem that if the great and crying cause of grievance, which had so long agitated and divided the public mind were once removed, there would be no powerful rallying cry for the disaffected, and that in any dangerous crisis the Government would find all reasonable men in Ireland and all men in England by its side.

He saw, however, more clearly than most people, and in fact it was this foresight that had made him so long the opponent of the measure which he had recently advocated, that to bring the Irish Catholics into Parliament was the eventual transfer of power from the Protestant to the Catholic.

The great policy would, no doubt, have been to accept at once this consequence in its full extent, and to have conciliated the Catholic majority, and the Catholic priesthood, by abandoning everything which under a Protestant ascendancy had been established. But no one was prepared for this. The Whigs would have opposed it as well as the Tories. The English Protestant Church would have made common cause with the Irish Protestant Church,—the English Protestants in general with the Irish Protestants. In short, it was not practicable at the moment on which our attention had been hitherto concentrated to do more for the Irish Catholics than had been done; and this was not likely, as Mr. Peel himself had said in 1817, to satisfy them: "We entered, therefore, inadvertently on a period of transition, in which a series of new difficulties were certain to be the result of the removal of the one great difficulty." Under such circumstances, Mr. Peel conceived he had only to watch events; it was not in accordance with the natural tendency of his character to anticipate them, and to act in the different situations that might arise as a practical view of each particular situation might suggest.

He was right, no doubt, in considering that the Catholic Relief Bill would not realise the expectations of its most ardent supporters, and it must be added that the state of things amidst which it was passed was alone sufficient to destroy many of those expectations. Agitation had evidently obtained for Ireland what loyalty and forbearance had never procured; and though the fear to which our statesmen had yielded might be what Lord Palmerston asserted, "the provident mother of safety," a concession to it, however wise or timely, gave a very redoubtable force to the menacing spirit by which concession had been gained. That force remained with all its elements perfectly organized, and in the hands of a man whom it was equally difficult to have for a friend or an enemy.

His violence shocked your more timid friends if he supported you, and encouraged your more timid enemies if he attacked you.

The Government, which had in reality yielded to him, did not wish to appear to have done so. It consequently provoked an altercation which it might as well have avoided. Mr. O'Connell had been returned for Clare, when by law he could not sit in Parliament, but when by law he could be elected. It was not unfair to say his election should not give him a seat in Parliament, because when he was elected he could not have a seat. But, on the other hand, it might be contended that, having been elected legally, he was entitled to take his seat when no legal impediment prevented it. The better policy would doubtless have been, not to fight a personal battle after having yielded in the public contest.

The Government, however, compelled Mr. O'Connell to undergo a new election; and considering this a declaration of war, he adopted a tone of hostility to the Ministry, far too extravagant to do them harm in England, but which added greatly to their difficulties in Ireland,— where a thorough social disorganization rendered the Government impotent for the protection of property and life against robbery and murder, unless it could count amongst its allies patriotism and popularity themselves.

But besides the weakness of the Government in Ireland, it was generally weak, for it had lost by the change in its Irish policy much of its previous support, and could hardly hope to maintain itself any length of time without getting back former partisans, or drawing closer to new allies.

To regain friends whom you have once lost, owing to a violent difference on a great political principle, is an affair neither easily nor rapidly managed. It requires agreement on some question as important as that which created disagreement.

On the other hand, for the Tories, under the Duke of Wellington, to have coalesced with the Whigs, under Lord Grey, called for sacrifices on both sides too great to be accepted by either with honour or even propriety.

The Duke of Wellington and Mr. Peel tried, therefore, a moderate course. Detaching able men from the Whig ranks where they could secure them, carrying out administrative reforms, opposing constitutional changes, doing, in short, all which could be done to conciliate one party without further alienating another, and carrying on affairs, as in quiet times a despotic Government can do, even with credit and popularity. But a free Government rarely admits, for any lengthened period, of this even and tranquil course; it generates energies and passions that must be employed, and which concentrate in an opposition to the rulers who do not know how to employ them.

Some administrative improvements were nevertheless worthy of notice. The watchman's staff was broken in the metropolis. The criminal code was still further improved, and punishment by death in cases of forgery partially abolished and generally discountenanced.

Taxes also were repealed, and savings boasted of. But the nation had become used to strong political excitement, and had a sort of instinct that the passing of the Roman Catholic Bill should be followed by some marked and general policy, analogous to the liberal spirit which had dictated that measure.

Nor was this all. Mr. Canning, when he said that he would not serve under a military premier, had expressed an English feeling. The Duke of Wellington's treatment of Mr. Huskisson was too much like that of a general who expects implicit obedience from his inferior officers. The very determination he had displayed in disregarding and overruling George IV.'s anti-Catholic prejudices, evinced a resolve to be obeyed that seemed to many dangerous. His strong innate sense of superiority, the language, calm and decided, in which it was displayed, were not to the taste of our public in a soldier at the head of affairs, though they might have pleased in a civilian. At the same time, this undisguised and unaffected superiority lowered his colleagues in the public estimation, whilst the general tendency of many minds is to refuse one order of ability where they admit another.

An act of foreign policy, moreover, did the administration at this time an immense injury. We had cordially, though indirectly, placed Donna Maria on the throne of Portugal, and endowed that country with a constitution. Don Miguel, Donna Maria's uncle, afterwards dispossessed her of that throne and ruled despotically. We had not, however, as yet recognised him as the Portuguese Sovereign. We still honoured the niece residing in England with that title, when an incident occurred which led to grave doubts as to whether the great commander was also a great minister.

The Island of Terceira still acknowledged Donna Maria's sway; and an expedition, consisting chiefly of her own subjects, had embarked from Portsmouth for that Island, when it was stopped and prevented from landing there by a British naval force, the pretext being that the expedition, though first bound to Terceira, was going to be sent to Portugal, and to be employed against Don Miguel.

But no sufficient proof was given of this intention; the force arrested in its passage was a Portuguese force, proceeding to a place *bonâ fide* in the Queen of Portugal's possession. If it were eventually to be landed on the territory held by the usurper, it had not yet made manifest that such was its destination. Its object might be merely to defend Terceira, which had lately been attacked. Arguments might be drawn from international law both for and against our conduct. But the public did not go into these arguments; what it saw was, that Mr. Canning had favoured the constitutional cause, that the Duke of Wellington was favouring the absolute one. "He did not do this," said people "to please his own nation; no one suspected him of doing it to gratify a petty tyrant. He did it then to satisfy the great potentates of the

Continent who were adverse to freedom." This suspicion, not founded on fact, but justified by appearances, weighed upon the Cabinet as to its whole foreign policy, and reacted upon its policy at home.

So strong were its effects, that when Charles X. called Prince Polignac to the head of his counsels, it was said, "Oh, this is the Duke of Wellington's doing!" and even when the ordinances of July were published, it was supposed that they had been advised by our military premier. Feelings of this sort have no limit. They spread like a mist over opinion.

At this time occurred the death of George IV. (June 26th, 1830), and a new era opened in our history.

William IV., who succeeded, had not the same talents or accomplishments as the deceased monarch, his brother, nor perhaps the same powers of mind. But he was more honest and straightforward; took a greater interest in the welfare of the nation, and was very desirous to be beloved by his people. He retained the same Ministry, but a new reign added to the impression that there must ere long be a new Cabinet, and the circumstances under which the forthcoming elections took place confirmed this impression. Parliament was dissolved on the 23rd of July, and on the 30th was proclaimed the triumph of a revolution in Paris; whilst immediately after the fall of the throne of Charles X. came that general crash of dynasties which shook the nerves of every prince in Europe.

The roar of revolution abroad did not resound in England and obscure the lustre of the brightest reputations; nevertheless, it was echoed in a general cry, for constitutional change, and accompanying this cry, there was, as winter approached, an almost general alarm from the demoralization that prevailed in the rural districts and the excitement that existed in the great towns.

The country wanted to be reassured and calmed. The King's speech (Nov. 2, 1830) was not calculated to supply this want. With respect to home affairs, it spoke of the dangerous state of Ireland, and said nothing of the one question which began to occupy men's minds in England—the question of Reform. Abroad, our policy had been weak against Russia when on her road to Constantinople; timid and uncertain towards Greece, when the time was come for her recognition; and now we announced the intention of opening diplomatic relations with Don Miguel, in Portugal, and made the insurrection in Belgium popular by taking the King of the Netherlands under our protection.

In short, there was hardly one word our new Sovereign was made to say which did not add to the unpopularity of his ministers. These ministers, indeed, were in a critical position.

Some plan of Parliamentary Reform had of necessity to be proposed. The true Conservative policy would have been to propose a moderate plan before increased disquietude suggested a violent one. Nor was this task a difficult one at that moment; for if a Parliamentary Reform was proclaimed necessary, there was no definite idea as to what that Reform should be. Many of the Tories were willing to give Representatives to a few of the great towns, and to diminish in some degree the number of close boroughs; a large portion of the Whigs would have been satisfied with a Reform on this basis.

It is probable that Sir Robert Peel (Mr. Peel had succeeded to his father's title in March of this year), would have inclined, had he been completely his own master, towards some course of this kind.

But, whilst a general incertitude prevailed as to

what would be the best course for the Government to pursue, the Duke of Wellington, who felt convinced that we should be led step by step to revolution if we did not at once and decidedly declare against all change, determined to check any contrary disposition in his followers before it was expressed, and surprised all persons by the declaration that the Constitution as it stood was perfect, and that no alteration in it would be proposed as long as he was Prime Minister.

I have reason to believe that his more wary colleague was by no means pleased with this hasty and decided announcement; and, although he could not directly contradict the speech of his chief, he in a certain degree mitigated its effect by saying: "That he did not at present see any prospect of such a measure of safe, moderate Reform as His Majesty's Government *might be inclined to sanction*," which, in fact, said that if a moderate, safe Reform were found, it would be sanctioned. But the party in office, after the significant words of the Premier, were compromised; and the line they had to follow practically traced.

Those words were hazardous and bold; but in times of doubt and peril, boldness has sometimes its advantages. One must not, however, be bold with any appearance of timidity. But the Government was about to show that it wanted that resosolution which was its only remaining protection.

The King had been invited to dine with the Lord Mayor on the 9th of November. There are always a great many busy people on such occasions who think of making themselves important by giving information, and the Lord Mayor is precisely the person who is most brought into contact with these people. It is not in the least surprising, therefore, that his Lordship was told there was a plot for attacking the Duke of Wellington on his way to the city, and that he had better be well guarded. On this somewhat trumpery story, and not very awful warning, the Government put off the Royal dinner, saying, they feared a tumult.

It is evident that a set of Ministers so unpopular that they thought they could not safely accompany the sovereign through the City of London to the Mansion House, were not the men to remain in office in a time of trouble and agitation. Thus, the days of the Government were now numbered; and being on the 15th of November in a minority of 29, on a motion respecting the arrangements of the civil list, they resigned.

Lord Grey succeeded the Duke of Wellington,

and announced his intention of bringing forward a measure of Reform.

I had been elected for that Parliament, and returned from abroad but a few days after the change of Government.

I then saw Sir Robert Peel for the first time, and it was impossible, after attending three or four sittings of the House of Commons, not to have one's attention peculiarly attracted to him.

He was tall and powerfully built. His body somewhat bulky for his limbs, his head small and well-formed, his features regular. His countenance was not what would be generally called expressive, but it was capable of taking the expression he wished to give it, humour, sarcasm, persuasion, and command, being its alternate characteristics. The character of the man was seen more, however, in the whole person than in the face. He did not stoop, but he bent rather forwards; his mode of walking was peculiar, and rather like that of a cat, but of a cat that was well acquainted with the ground it was moving over; the step showed no doubt or apprehension, it could hardly be called stealthy, but it glided on firmly and cautiously, without haste, or swagger, or unevenness, and, as he quietly walked from the bar to his seat, he looked round him, as if scanning the assembly, and when anything particular was expected, sat down with an air of preparation for the coming contest.

The oftener you heard him speak the more his speaking gained upon you. Addressing the House several times in the night on various subjects, he always seemed to know more than any one else knew about each of them, and to convey to you the idea that he thought he did so. His language was not usually striking, but it was always singularly correct, and gathered force with the development of his argument. He never seemed occupied with himself. His effort was evidently directed to convince you, not that he was *eloquent*, but that he was *right*. When the subject suited it, he would be witty, and with a look and a few words he could most effectively convey contempt; he could reply also with great spirit to an attack, but he was rarely aggressive. He seemed rather to aim at gaining the doubtful, than mortifying or crushing the hostile. His great rivals, Canning and Brougham, being removed, he no doubt felt more at his ease than formerly; and though there was nothing like assumption or pretension in his manner, there was a tone of superiority, which he justified by a great store of knowledge, a clear and impressive style, and a constant readiness to discuss any question that arose.

Lord John Russell had not then the talents for debate which he subsequently displayed. Lord Palmerston had only made one or two great speeches. Sir James Graham was chiefly remarkable for a weighty statement. Mr. Charles Grant had lost his once great oratorical powers. Mr. Macaulay was only beginning to deliver his marvellous orations. O'Connell, mighty to a mob, was not in his place when addressing a refined and supercilious audience. Mr. Stanley, the late Lord Derby, surpassed Sir R. Peel and every one else in vivacity, wit, lucidity, and energy. But he struck you more as a first-rate cavalry officer than as a commander-in-chief. Sir Robert, cool and self-collected, gave you, on the contrary, the idea of a great, prudent, wary leader who was fighting after a plan, and keeping his eye during the whole of the battle directed to the result. You felt, at least I felt, that without being superior to many of his competitors as a man, he was far superior to all as a Member of Parliament; and his ascendancy was the more visible as the whole strength of his party was in him.

He profited, no doubt, by the fact that the

Whigs had been (with the exception of a short interval) out of office for nearly half a century, and showed at every step the self-sufficiency of men of talent, and the incapacity of men without experience. Every one felt, indeed, that in the ordinary course of things their official career would be short, and none were more convinced of this than their leaders. They acted accordingly. Under any circumstances they were pledged to bring forward a Reform Bill; but under actual circumstances their policy was to bring forward a Reform Bill that would render it almost impossible for their probable successors to deal with that question. Such a Bill they introduced, destroying at one swoop sixty small boroughs, and taking one member from forty-seven more.

Mr. John Smith, an ardent Reformer, said that the Government measure went so far beyond his expectations, that it took away his breath. I myself happened to meet Mr. Hunt, the famous Radical of those days, in the tea-room of the House of Commons, just before Lord John Russell rose. We had some conversation on the project about to be proposed, no one out of a small circle having any conception as to what it would be. Mr. Hunt said, if it gave members to a few of the great towns, and disfranchised with compensation a few close boroughs, the public would rest contented for the moment with this concession. In fact, the Government plan was received with profound astonishment. Lord John continued his explanations of it amidst cheers and laughter. It almost appeared a joke; and had Sir Robert Peel risen when Lord John sat down, and said that "he had been prepared to consider any reasonable or practical plan, but that the plan of the Government was a mockery repugnant to the good sense of the House, and that he could not therefore allow the time of Parliament to be lost by discussing it; moving at the same time the order of the day, and pledging himself to bring the question in a practical form under the attention of the House of Commons at an early opportunity," he would have had a majority of at least a hundred in his favour.

It was a great occasion for a less prudent man. But Sir Robert Peel was not an improvisatore in action, though he was in words. He required time to prepare a decision. He was moreover fettered by his relations with the late premier. Could he reject at once a project of Reform, however absurd, without taking up the question of Reform? Could he pledge his party to take up that question without being certain of his party's pretty general acquiescence?

He persuaded himself, not unnaturally, that the Government measure had no chance of success; that nothing would be lost by an appearance of moderation, and that time would thus be gained for the Opposition to combine its plans.

Nine men out of ten would have judged the matter as he did, and been wrong as he was. But the magnitude of the Whig measure, which appeared at the moment its weakness, was in reality its strength. It roused the whole country.

Much, also, in a crisis like the one through which the country had now to pass, depends on the action of individuals whose names are not always found in history. There happened, at the moment of which I am speaking, to be a man connected with the Whig Government who, by his frank, good-natured manner, his knowledge of human nature, his habits of business, his general acquaintance with all classes of persons, and his untiring activity, gave an intensity and a direction to the general sentiment which it would not otherwise have attained.

I allude to Mr. Edward Ellice, Secretary of the Treasury. He was emphatically a man of the world, having lived with all classes of it. His intellect was clear, and adapted to business; and he liked that sort of business which brought him into contact with men. Naturally kind-hearted and good-natured, with frank and easy manners, he entered into other people's plans and feelings, and left every one with the conviction that he had been speaking to a friend who at the proper time would do him a service. He took upon himself the management of the Press, and was entrusted shortly afterwards (when Lord Grey, finding his ministry in a minority in the House of Commons, obtained the King's permission to dissolve Parliament) with the management of the elections. He knew that the great danger to a Reform party is almost always division, and bound the Reform party on that occasion together by the cry of " The bill! the whole bill, and nothing but the bill!"

All argument, all discussion, all objection, were absorbed by this overwhelming cry, which repeated from one end of the country to another, drowned the voice of criticism, and obliged every one to take his place either as an advocate of the Government measure, or an opponent of the popular will.

The general feeling, when, after the elections in 1831, the shattered forces of the Tory party gathered in scanty array around their distinguished leader, was that that party was no more, or at least had perished, as far as the possession of political power was concerned, for the next twenty years. People did not sufficiently recognize the changeful vibration of opinion; neither did they take sufficiently into account the fact that there will always, in a state like ours, be a set of men who wish to make the institutions more democratic, and a set of men who do not wish this; though at different epochs the battle for or against democracy will be fought on different grounds. The Reform Bill now proposed having been once agreed to, it was certain that there would again be persons for further changes, and persons against them. Sir Robert's great care, therefore, when our old institutions sunk, was not to cling to them so fast as to sink with them. He defended, then, the opinions he had heretofore asserted, but he defended them rather as things that had been good, and were gone by, than as things that were good and which could be maintained. The Tories in the House of Lords were in a more difficult position than the Tories in the House of Commons. They were called upon to express their opinions, and to do so conscientiously. They were in a majority in the upper assembly, as the Whigs were in a majority in the lower one. According to the theory of the Constitution the vote of one branch of the Legislature was as valid as that of the other. Were they to desert their duties, and declare they were incompetent to discharge them? They considered they were not. They, therefore, threw out the Government bill when it was brought before them for decision, and thus it had again to be introduced into the House of Commons. Again it arrived at the House of Lords, which displayed a disposition to reject it once more.

Lord Grey, in this condition of things, asked the King for the power of making peers, or for the permission to retire from his Majesty's service. His resignation was accepted, and the Duke of Wellington was charged with forming a new Government, which was to propose a new Reform Bill. He applied to Sir Robert Peel for assistance, but Sir Robert saw that the moment for him to deal with the question of Reform was passed, and declined to give that assistance, saying that he was not the proper person to represent a compromise. That any Reform Bill that would now satisfy the momentary excitement must comprehend changes that he believed would be permanently injurious.

He felt, indeed, that it would be better to let the reformers carry their own bill than to bring forward another bill which could not greatly differ from the one which the House of Commons had already sanctioned, and which, nevertheless, would not satisfy, because it would be considered the bill of the House of Lords. The Duke of Wellington consequently was obliged to retire, the Lords to give way. Lord Grey's Reform Bill was carried, and Sir Robert Peel took his seat in a new Parliament formed by his opponents, who thought they had secured thereby the permanence of their own power.

SIR ROBERT PEEL.

PART V.

Effects of Reform.—Changes produced by Reform.—Daniel O'Connell.—Lord Melbourne.—Choice of Speaker.—The Irish Tithe Bill.—Measures of Lord Melbourne.—The Irish Question.—The Queen's Household.—The Corn Law League.—Whig Measures.

SIR ROBERT PEEL.

PART V.

FROM THE REFORMED PARLIAMENT IN 1832, TO THE PEEL MINISTRY IN 1843.

I.

THE great measure just passed into law was not calculated to justify the fears of immediate and violent consequences; but was certain to produce gradual and important changes.

The new constitution breathed, in fact, a perfectly different spirit from the old one. The vitality of our former government was drawn from the higher classes and the lower ones. An election for Westminster was not merely the return of two members to Parliament: it was a manifestation of the feeling prevalent amongst the masses throughout England; and the feeling amongst the masses had a great influence in moments of excitement, and in all matters touching the national dignity and honour. On the other hand, it was by the combinations of powerful families that a majority was formed in Parliament, which, in ordinary times, and when no great question was at issue, ruled the country.

The populace, by its passions—the aristocracy, by its pride—gave energy to the will, and elevation to the character of the nation, disposing it to enterprise and to action. The Government we had recently created was, on the contrary, filled with the soul of the middle classes, which is not cast in an heroic mould. Its objects are material, its interests are involved in the accidents of the moment. What may happen in five years to a man in trade, is of comparatively small consequence. What may happen immediately, makes or mars his fortunes. Moreover, the persons likely to replace the young men, distinguished for their general abilities and general instruction, who had formerly represented the smaller boroughs, were now for the most part elderly men with a local reputation, habits already acquired, and without the knowledge, the energy, or the wish to commence a new career as politicians.

A writer on Representative Government has said, that the two important elements to represent are intellect and numbers, because they are the two great elements of force. The new Reform Bill did not affect especially to represent either. But it represented peace, manufactures, expediency, practical acquaintance with particular branches of trade. It established a greater reality. A member of Parliament was more likely to represent a real thing concerning the public than a mere idea concerning it. The details of daily business were more certain to be attended to, useless wars to be put on one side.

On the other hand, that high spirit which insensibly sustains a powerful nation, that devotion to the permanent interests of the country, which leads to temporary sacrifices for its character and prestige, that extensive and comprehensive knowledge of national interests, which forms statesmen, and is the peculiar attribute of an enlightened and patriotic aristocracy, that generous sympathy with what is right, and detestation for what is wrong, which exists nowhere with such intensity as in the working classes, who are swayed more by sentiment, and less by calculation, than any other class—all those qualities, in short, which make one state, without our being able exactly to say why, dominate morally and physically over other states, were somewhat too feebly implanted in our new institutions; and these institutions generated a set of politicians who, with a very limited range of view, denied the existence of principles that were beyond the scope of their observation.

There were also other considerations, probably overlooked by those who imagined they were building up a permanent system by the bill of 1832. The middle class, which is perhaps the most important one for a government to conciliate, is not a class that can itself govern. Its temporary rule nearly always leads to a democracy or to a despotism; it must, therefore, be considered as a mere step, upwards or downwards, in a new order of things. Besides, if you destroy traditional respect, and that kind of instinct of obedience which is created by the habit of obeying spontaneously to-morrow, what you obeyed without inquiry yesterday—if you begin by condemning everything in a constitution which reason does not approve, you must arrive at a constitution which reason will sanction. You cannot destroy anomalies and preserve anomalies. The tide of innovation which you have directed towards the one anomaly as absurd, will, ere long, sweep away, as equally ridiculous, another anomaly. There is no solid resting place between custom and argument. What is no longer defended by the one, must be made defensible by the other.

It is only by degrees, however, that the full extent of a great change developes itself; for the peculiarities of a new constitution are always modified when that new constitution is carried out by men who have grown up under the preceding one; and in the meantime the vessel of the State, struggling between old habits and new ideas, must be exposed to the action of changeful and contrary winds.

Thus, the Reform party, temporarily united during the recent combat, split into several sections at its termination.

First, Lord Durham quitted the administration, because he thought it too cautious; secondly, Mr. Stanley and Sir James Graham quitted it, because they each thought it too fast; finally, Lord Grey himself quitted it, because he deemed that his authority was diminishing, as his generation was dying away, and younger men absorbing old influences. In the meantime Mr. O'Connell continued to be a great embarrassment. He represented the majority of the Irish people, who contended for a supremacy over the minority, a contest in which it was natural for the Catholics to engage after they had been declared as good citizens as the Protestants; but in which it was impossible for the British Government to concur, so long as there was a feud between the Protestant and the Catholic, and that the Protestant majority in England were disposed to sustain the Protestant minority in Ireland.

Hence, the reformed Parliament had met amidst cries for the repeal of the Union, and those savage violations of social order which, in the sister kingdom, are the usual attendants on political agitation.

The Ministry first tried coercion, but its effects could only be temporary, and they alienated a portion of its supporters. It then tried conciliation. But it was found impossible to conciliate the Irish Catholics without conciliating their leader. That leader was not irreconcilable, for he was vain: and vain men may always be managed by managing their vanity; but to gratify the vanity of a man who was always defying the power of England, was to mortify the pride of the English people.

Lord Melbourne had succeeded Lord Grey. He united various accomplishments with a manly understanding and a character inclined to moderation. There could not have been selected a statesman better qualified to preside over a Cabinet containing conflicting opinions and antagonistic ambitions. But no body of men, acting together under a system of compromises, can act with vigour or maintain authority. All these circumstances gave an air of feebleness and inferiority to an administration which contained, nevertheless, many men of superior ability. But that, perhaps, which tended most to discredit the ministry, was the credit which Sir Robert Peel was daily gaining as its opponent.

Carefully separating himself from the extreme opinions to be found in his own party, condemning merely the extreme opinions on the opposite one; professing the views and holding the language of a mediator between opinions that found no longer an echo in the public mind, and opinions that had not yet been ripened by public approbation; contrasting by his clear and uniform line of conduct with the apparent variations and vacillations of a Cabinet that was alternately swayed by diverging tendencies; professing no desire for power, he created by degrees a growing opinion that he was the statesman who ought to possess it: and thus, when the Reform Ministry had to add to its former losses that of Lord Althorpe, who by the death of Lord Spencer was withdrawn from the

House of Commons, which he had long led with a singular deficiency in the powers of debate, but with the shrewdness and courtesy of a man of the world, the King thought himself justified in removing a Cabinet which he considered deficient in dignity, spirit, and consideration.

The Duke of Wellington, to whom he offered the post of Premier, declined it, and recommended Sir Robert Peel. Sir Robert had not expected, nor perhaps wished for, so sudden a summons. He was, in fact, at Rome when he was offered, for the first time, the highest place in the Cabinet. Returning to England instantly, he accepted the offer. His object now was to organise a new Conservative party on a new basis, and to come forward himself as a new man in a new state of affairs, neither lingering over ancient pledges nor fettered by previous declarations. As the first necessity for a new system, he sought new men, and wishing to obliterate the prejudice against himself as an anti-Reformer by a union with those who had been Reformers, hastened to invite Sir James Graham and Lord Stanley to join him. This invitation being declined, he had to fall back on his former associates; but being unable to change the furniture of the old Conservative Cabinet, he repainted and regilded it. In a letter to the electors of Tamworth, which engrafted many liberal promises on Conservative principles, he went as far towards gaining new proselytes as was compatible with retaining old adherents. This letter was a preparation for the great struggle on the hustings which was now about to take place. Parliament had been dissolved, and the appeal made to the country was answered by the addition of one hundred members to the new Conservative party. Such an addition was sufficient to justify King William's belief that a considerable change had taken place in public opinion, but was not sufficient to give a majority in the House of Commons to the ministry he had chosen. It was beaten by ten votes on the choice of a Speaker, Mr. Abercrombie having that majority over Mr. Manners Sutton.

But if Sir Robert Peel had not a sufficient majority to insure his maintenance in office, the Whigs were not so sure of a majority as to risk a direct attempt to turn him out, unless on some specific case which called for a vote to sanction a specific opinion. Sir Robert's policy was to avoid a case of this kind, knowing that, if he could once by his tact, prudence, and ability, increase his numbers and establish a tendency in his favour, the fluctuating and uncertain would soon join his standard. This policy was contained in the speech with which he opened the campaign:

"With such prospects I feel it to be my duty—my first and paramount duty—to maintain the post which has been confided to me, and to stand by the trust which I did not seek, but which I could not decline. I call upon you not to condemn before you have heard — to receive at least the measures I shall propose—to amend them if they are defective—to extend them if they fall short of your expectations; but at least to give me the opportunity of presenting them, that you yourselves may consider and dispose of them. I make great offers, which should not be lightly rejected! I offer you the prospect of continued peace—the restored confidence of powerful states, that are willing to seize the opportunity of reducing great armies, and thus diminishing the chances of hostile collision. I offer you reduced estimates, improvements in civil jurisprudence, reform of ecclesiastical law, the settlement of the tithe question in Ireland, the commutation of the tithe in England, the removal of any real abuse in the Church, the redress of those grievances of which the Dissenters have any just grounds to complain. I offer you those specific measures, and I offer also to advance, soberly and cautiously, it is true, in the path of progressive improvement. I offer also the best chance that these things can be effected in willing concert with the other authorities of the State; thus restoring harmony, ensuring the maintenance, but not excluding the Reform (where Reform is really requisite) of ancient institutions."

It was difficult to use more seducing language, but the Opposition would not be seduced. From the 24th of February till the beginning of April, Sir Robert struggled against its unsparing attacks. It was not easy, however, to catch him exposed on any practical question; at last, however, he had to deal with one—he had promised to settle the tithe question in Ireland. How was he to do so? He thought to balk his assailants by bringing forward a measure this year very similar to one which they themselves had brought forward the year before. But once on Irish ground, he was pretty sure of being beaten. The difference between Lord John Russell and Mr. Stanley, which had led to the secession of the latter, was a difference of principle as to the nature of Church property: the former contending that if the revenue possessed by the Protestant Church in Ireland was larger than necessary for the decent maintenance of the Protestant clergy, the State might dispose of it as it thought proper; the latter asserting that the State could not employ it for any purposes that were not purely ecclesiastical.

This was a great question; it was brought to an issue in a very small manner. Lord John Russell proposed as a resolution that no Irish tithe bill would be satisfactory which did not contain a clause devoting any surplus over and above the requirements of the Church establishment to the purposes of secular education. A committee was then sitting to determine whether there was any such surplus as that alluded to or not, and it would have been, doubtless, more regular first to have got the surplus and then to have determined about its use. Besides, if it were to deal with so great a principle as the alienation of the property of the Protestant Church, it would surely have been worth while to do so for some great practical advantage. The majority, nevertheless, voted for Lord John Russell's proposition, partly because it established a public right, partly because it answered a party purpose. Thus Parliament decided against the inviolability of Church property—a decision certain to affect the future; which did affect the present; and Sir Robert Peel was forced to resign the seals of the Treasury.

But let us be just. Never did a statesman enter office more triumphantly than Sir Robert Peel left it. His self-confidence, his tact, his general knowledge, his temper, filled even his opponents with admiration!

It was impossible not to acknowledge to oneself that there was a man who seemed shaped expressly for being first minister of England. But, on the other hand, a sense of justice compelled one to consider that Lord Melbourne had done nothing to justify the manner in which he had been dismissed; that the party he represented had but two years since achieved a popular triumph which rendered the reign of William IV. almost as memorable in our annals as that of William III.—that it had added to this triumph, in the name of Liberty, a triumph quite as great in the cause of Humanity; and that it would have inflicted a stigma of fickleness on our national character to pass by with indifference and neglect the author of the Reform Bill and the Negro Emancipation Bill—condemning a party still possessed of a majority in the most important branch of the Legislature, on the ground that the late Earl of Spencer was no more, and that it was necessary to replace Lord Althorpe— an honest man of respectable talents—by Lord John Russell—an honest man of very eminent talents.

Sir Robert's attempt, in fact, though made bravely and sustained with consummate ability, was premature; made a few years later,—when the Stanley party had joined and were conformed with the Peel party, and made in consequence of some parliamentary measure, not as the consequence, which it then appeared to be, of Royal patronage and favour,—the result would have been different.

At the same time, it made an immense change in the condition of the Tory party. That party, after this attempt, was no longer a shattered band of impossible politicians, placed by public opinion without the pale of political power.

It became a compact, numerous, and hopeful party, considered by the country as prudent and practical, and having at its head the man most looked up to in that House of Parliament, which he declared publicly he would never quit.

For four years after this struggle Sir Robert Peel remained at the head of the powerful opposition he had gradually collected around him; the Whig Government having in the meantime to perform the very difficult and ungrateful task of carrying out changes which it deemed necessary, against Conservatives, and opposing innovations which it deemed dangerous, against Reformers. The friends of Liberal institutions and of religious toleration, and even of administrative improvement, owe it a debt of gratitude which they have never fully paid. The introduction of popular suffrage into the system of municipal government; the removal of various grievances that still existed and were mortifying and harassing to the Dissenters; the reduction of newspaper stamps; the commutation of tithes, are the footprints which Lord Melbourne's administration left on those times. On the other hand, Lord John Russell resisted in its name vote by ballot (a question of which both its advocates and opponents exaggerated the importance); any further extension of the suffrage, and also the re-establishment of triennial Parliaments. His great antagonist aided him in respect to all measures which the public, irrespective of parties, were prepared to adopt, and supported him against all demands which the more democratic portion of his adherents put forward, but depreciated his general authority by showing that, though invested with the functions of Government, he and his colleagues had not the power of governing.

The great battle-field, however, between Whig and Tory, or as the latter now called themselves "Conservatives," was, as it had long been and seems always destined to be,—Ireland; for there was still to settle that Irish Tithes Bill, into which the Whigs had insisted for some time on inserting the principle of appropriation; and there was also another question at stake, more pressing and more practical,—that of the Irish corporations.

The Whigs were for applying to the municipalities in Ireland the same principles of popular election which had been applied to municipalities in England and Scotland. The Conservatives contended that Irish society was not constituted like English and Scotch society, and would not admit of the same institutions. They urged that the old municipalities had been constituted on the basis most proper to keep up an exclusive Protestant ascendancy; they contended that the new municipalities according to the Government plan, seemed likely to create an exclusive ascendancy for the Catholics; and they asserted that under such circumstances it would be wise and just to establish an order of things that would preserve some balance between the two great divisions of the Irish community. They entered, in fact, upon that difficult ground, a ground made difficult when the Irish Catholic was placed on an equality with the Irish Protestant, and commenced the transfer of power from a long predominant minority to an ambitious and irritated majority. But it was after carefully weighing immediate peril against contingent difficulties, that Sir Robert Peel had already taken his choice; and he ought now to have accepted its consequences. The worst way of arguing for a legislative union between two countries is surely to question that they will admit of the same laws? The best way of removing religious passions from political affairs, is to forget in political questions religious distinctions.

By not acting on these convictions, he re-opened the sore which he had made such sacrifices to heal, but this error, which was certain to bear its punishment in regard to Ireland at a later season, did not affect his immediate position in the rest of the Empire.

II.

We have said that anything like an alliance with a man who assumed an attitude of defiance towards English power would arouse the instincts of English pride. Besides, nothing at all times injures and lowers a government more than the appearance of being counselled by a private individual who is not publicly responsible for his advice. The mere fact that the Whig policy was more congenial to Mr. O'Connell's views than the Tory one, would have naturally created a sort of link between this singular man and the Whig Government. To keep his followers together, he wanted the influence of patronage; to obtain the aid of his followers, the Government did not show itself unwilling to bestow patronage upon him. In the meantime the independence of his attitude and language—an independence which the peculiarity of his position obliged him somewhat ostentatiously to display—apparently justified the accusation that the Premier was his *protégé*, and not he the *protégé* of the Premier. Hence, though the House of Commons still maintained by a small majority the Whig policy in Ireland, there was a growing coolness amongst the English at large towards Irish grievances, and a disposition to accuse Lord Melbourne of a mean desire to retain place, when in reality he was undergoing many personal mortifications from public motives.

The Conservatives in Parliament had, moreover, increased, and were become impatient. A difference between the Colonial Office and the Jamaica Legislature offered the opportunity of adding some votes to that number. A battle was fought, and the ministry only gained a majority of five. Being oppressed by a long catalogue of questions which it had undertaken to settle, and had not the power to deal with, the Ministry not unwillingly resigned; and, by the Duke of Wellington's advice, Sir Robert Peel had the same commission confided to him by Queen Victoria which he had received previously from William IV.

A difficulty, however, here intervened with respect to certain leaders in the highest position at Court, whom the Premier desired to remove, and from whom the Queen would not consent to part. The question ought not to have arisen, but once having done so, concession could not be made with becoming dignity, either by the sovereign or by the statesman, who had acted too much as a man of business, and too little as a man of the world.

III.

Lord Melbourne resumed for a time the position he had abandoned, but, by doing so, he rather weakened than strengthened his party, and gave his opponents the advantage of maturing their strength by a prolonged contest against a ministry which had confessed its incapacity to master the difficulties which beset it.

These difficulties were not a little increased by combinations which betokened an insurrectionary disposition amongst the working classes, who, in some cases, proceeded to riot, and set forth their general plans and devises on the project of a constitution called "the people's charter," a project which was generally considered as subversive of credit, property, and order.

The Conservatives attributed these doctrines, however denounced by the Whigs, as deducible from Whig tendencies, and profited by the mistrust which a weak government and an agitated commonalty naturally suggested. One hostile motion succeeded another, each manifesting an increasing decline in the strength of the Whigs, and an increasing confidence on the part of their opponents, until a new opportunity arose for bringing together the same parties that had, by their union, brought about Lord Melbourne's previous resignation.

The doctrines of Free Trade had of late made rapid progress; they were principally directed by the Corn Law League, recently established, towards a free trade in corn, and against a free trade in this commodity Sir Robert Peel had emphatically declared himself; but they were also applicable to all articles of commerce, and to the general principles of Free Trade in dealing with the greater number of these articles the Conservative leader gave his assent. As, however, he made an exception with respect to corn, so he made an exception as to sugar; his argument being, that the state of our West Indian colonies merited our special consideration, for we had deprived them of slave labour, and thereby placed them in an unequal condition as to their products with countries which employed slave labour.

For this inequality, he said, it is fair that you should compensate by imposing a heavier duty on sugar produced by slave labour than on the sugar cultivated by free labour. The Government, on the other hand, not daring as yet to declare decidedly in favour of a Free Trade in corn, was disposed to lower and fix the duty, which was then variable, and to abolish the differential duties on timber and sugar. In this state of things, Lord Sandon gave the following notice :—" That, considering the efforts and sacrifices which Parliament and the country have made for the abolition of the slave trade and slavery, with the earnest hope that their exertions and example might lead to a mitigation and final extinction of those evils in other countries, this House is not prepared (especially with the present prospect of the supply of sugar from the British possessions) to adopt the measure proposed by her Majesty's Government, for the reduction of the duty on foreign sugar."

After a long debate, the opposition had a

majority of thirty-six. The ministers did not resign, meaning to dissolve, but intending first to renovate their claims to public sympathy by an exposition of Free Trade policy, which, though it might not go so far as Mr. Cobden and his friends might desire, would still go far enough to place them at the head of the movement which they foresaw would soon agitate the country.

Sir Robert, however, little disposed after his recent victory to afford a respite to his adversaries, declaring that he did not think it for the advantage of the monarchy that the servants of the Crown should be retained, when unable to carry those measures which they felt it their duty to advise, moved, on the 27th of May, a vote of want of confidence, and obtained a majority of one. A dissolution followed, in which the party which still held office was more unsuccessful than could have been expected, and, at the opening of Parliament, ministers were in a minority of ninety-one. This closed their existence, but it might be recorded on their grave that they had finally given Ireland elective municipalities, and conferred on the three kingdoms the benefit of a penny postage.

SIR ROBERT PEEL.

PART VI.

Differences in the Country.—Sir Robert Peel's Programme.— A new Conservative Party.—Peel's Commercial Policy.—Catholic Education.—The Maynooth Grant.—Corn Law Agitation.—The Irish Distress.—Peel resumes the Government.—The Corn Laws repealed.—Review of Peel's career.—Character of Peel.—Peel and Canning contrasted.

SIR ROBERT PEEL.

PART VI.

FROM THE MINISTRY OF 1843 TO THE DEATH OF SIR ROBERT PEEL.

I.

THE great interest which attaches to Sir Robert Peel's life is derived from the period over which it extended, and his complete identification with the spirit and action of that period. It is difficult to point out in history any time at which such numerous changes in the character and Government of a country took place peacefully within so small a number of years. We are now at the sixth epoch in this remarkable career. The first ended by Mr. Peel's election for Oxford, and his quitting Ireland as the especial champion of the Protestant cause. The second, with his rupture with Lord Eldon, and his formation of a moderate administration, in which he stood as the mediator between extremes. The third, in which he effected the abrupt concession of the Catholic claims. The fourth, in which he opposed the reform or change in our system of representation. The fifth, in which, planting his standard on the basis of our new institutions, he carried into power the party most hostile to the principles on which those institutions had been remodelled. The sixth, as we shall see, concludes with the momentary destruction of that party.

The characteristic features of our Government when Mr. Peel began political life were the supremacy of Protestants, the peculiar and anomalous condition of nomination boroughs, and the predominant influence of our landed gentry. Such was what was called the English Constitution. The Protestant supremacy was, as a principle, abolished; the close boroughs were done away with; the landed influence was now beginning to be in jeopardy.

The elections that had just taken place were in some degree a trial of the comparative popularity of free trade and protectionist principles, the Protectionists being for the most part country gentlemen, voting generally with the Tories, and the Free Traders, who were chiefly from the mercantile and manufacturing classes, with the Whigs. But the opinions between the leaders of the two parties with respect to commercial principles were not so wide apart. Other causes affected their struggle for power.

The country had been for some time perplexed by the differences which prevailed amongst the liberals, and the discordant and heterogeneous elements of which their body was composed. It had a general idea that many of the questions under discussion were not ripe for a solution, that Sir Robert Peel, though adverse to change, was not blind to improvement; that his followers were more united than his opponents, and composed of a less adventurous class of politicians; above all, he himself considered that he was the person who, by his practical knowledge, was the most capable of restoring order to our finances, long since deranged by an annual deficit, which the late government had done nothing to supply. In short, the large majority in the country and in Parliament which brought Sir Robert Peel into office did so far more in homage to his personal prestige than in respect to the principles which his adherents represented. He stood, in fact, in the most eminent but in the most difficult position which an individual could occupy. It is worth while to consider what that position was.

From the time that the Reform Bill of 1832 had

been carried, in spite of the aristocratic branch of our Legislature, there had been a natural and continuous difference between the two Houses of Parliament, a difference that was in itself far more dangerous to the form of our constitution than any decision on any question on which they differed. In a celebrated speech which Sir R. Peel delivered at Merchant Tailors' Hall (in 1839) he had stated that his endeavour was to form such a party as might bring the House of Commons and the House of Lords into harmonious working. "My object," said he, "for some years past, has been to lay the foundations of a great party, which, existing in the House of Commons, and deriving its strength from the popular will, should diminish the risk and deaden the shock of collisions between the two deliberative branches of the Legislature." This could not be effected by a party which merely represented the feelings of the most democratic portion of the democratic assembly; it could still less be effected by a party only representing the feelings of the most aristocratic portion of the aristocratic assembly. A party was required that should draw strength from the moderate men of both assemblies. The Whigs had not been able to form a party of this kind; Sir Robert undertook to do so, stating then, and frequently afterwards, the course he should pursue with this object.

In Ireland he proposed to act up to the spirit of the Catholic Relief Bill, in his distribution of patronage to the Catholics, but to maintain the Protestant Church. In the rest of the empire he promised a careful attention to material interests and administrative reforms, and an unswerving opposition to further constitutional changes. As to commercial policy, he admitted the general theory of free trade, but contended that its application should be relative to existing circumstances and long-established interests, any sudden overthrow of which would interfere with the natural progress of events, and the gradual and safe development of national prosperity. For his own position he claimed an entire liberty, protesting that he did not mean to fetter the opinions of others, but that at the same time no consideration would induce him to carry out views or maintain opinions in which he did not concur.

"I do not estimate highly the distinction which office confers. To any man who is fit to hold it, its only value must be, not the patronage which the possessor is enabled to confer, but the opportunity which is offered to him of doing good to his country. And the moment I shall be convinced that that power is denied me, I tell every one who hears me that he confers on me no personal obligation in having placed me in this office. Free as the winds, I shall reserve to myself the power of retiring from the discharge of its onerous and harassing functions the moment I feel that I cannot discharge them with satisfaction to the public and to my own conscience."

This liberty he foresaw was necessary, for the object he had to effect was a compromise between conflicting extremes, in which he must expect to dissatisfy all those whose views were extreme. But it is public opinion which establishes extremes. What is extreme one day may not be so another. A certain latitude in accommodating himself to public opinion was therefore a natural claim.

But though Sir Robert Peel's intention was thus to form a new Conservative party, he was obliged to use old and recognized Conservative materials. The Protestants in Ireland, the country gentlemen in England, were the back bone of any Conservative party. He might endeavour to mitigate their prejudices and to popularize their opinions, but he could not have a Conservative party without them. The difficulties which this situation presented were not conspicuous when he had merely to criticise in opposition. They were certain, however, to become so when he began to act in office, and was exposed in his turn to criticism.

Years, however, had to pass before his plans could be developed or their tendency discovered. The distress was great; the finances were disordered; but the mere fact that Sir Robert Peel was at the head of affairs tranquillised the public mind. In this period, when confidence was required, the power of character was felt.

On the meeting of Parliament in the following year, the general scheme of the ministerial policy was explained. The intentions of the Government as to the corn trade were confined to the imposition of more moderate duties, graduating according to a sliding scale, which made the duty imposed depend on the average price of corn. The mode adopted for equalizing the revenue with the expenditure was an Income Tax, accompanied by a reduction in certain articles of consumption; and finally came a new tariff which had for its principal object the lowering the price of essential articles of food, and admitting raw materials applicable to manufactures. The proposed arrangements as to the corn duties were attacked by the Whigs, who were in favour of a fixed instead of a varying duty, and by the Free Traders, who contended that there should be no duties at all. It was attacked also by a certain number of country gentlemen, who considered that it afforded insufficient protection to land; but it was considered at the moment by the country at large as a tolerably fair compromise between conflicting demands. As to the Income Tax, it was submitted to as a disagreeable necessity, affording the simplest and surest method of rescuing the country from the degrading position of constant loans, whilst the tariff was hailed with general delight as increasing the value of income, thus affording a compensation for the reduction imposed on it.

It was on this tariff, indeed, the principles of which were gradually developed, that Sir Robert Peel's commercial policy was based. In the meantime the beneficial effects of his practical and active administration were soon apparent. The Poor Law was amended, a large saving was gained by the reduction of the Three and a Half per Cents., the currency was satisfactorily regulated by the Bank Charter Bill; the insolvent law was improved, above three millions of taxes were remitted. Here was fair subject for legitimate boast.

But whatever consideration these facts might procure for the Premier in the country, they did not add to his strength in the House of Commons, for there you can rarely conciliate opponents, whilst the appearance of an attempt to do so irritates supporters. It is true that the accusations brought against him by the Protectionists were as yet unjust. He had never declared himself a Protectionist in principle. From the days when Mr. Huskisson commenced his commercial policy he had accepted Mr. Huskisson's opinions. He had, to be sure, made some exceptions to the general theory which he then adopted, and these exceptions he still maintained. The persons interested in abolishing them declared at once that as the principles on which they might be defended had been disavowed, it was absurd that they should be afterwards maintained. The persons, however, who were interested in them, saw not only that they could not stand alone, but that they could not last long after the principles on which they had hitherto defended had been given up.

In the meantime, Ireland caused even more than its usual amount of disquietude and annoyance. Vague complaints violently expressed, monster meetings militarily organised, alarmed

K

the peaceful, encouraged the disaffected, and crushed all hopes of industrious tranquillity. The agitators demanded the repeal of the Union. The Government seized the arms of the peasantry. Mr. O'Connell and his son were arrested, and convicted by a jury on a charge of conspiracy, and though their sentence was subsequently set aside by the House of Lords, this exhibition of vigour produced some effect.

The perfect tranquillisation of Ireland, whether by Whig or Tory, is, I fear, impossible, until the united Legislature shall be disposed to give the majority in Ireland, under the restraint which the influence of property may justly create for the minority, what that majority would be able to obtain if Ireland had a Legislature of her own; but at the same time, the more the Imperial Government manifests its desire to conciliate those interests it cannot satisfy, the more it is likely to maintain in that long-distressed country a state of peace, if not of content.

Sir Robert Peel brought forward at this time a measure in conformity with these views. Up to the year 1795, the Catholic clergy had been in the habit of seeking their education abroad. The state of the continent at that time suggested the advisability of offering the means of such education within the British empire. It might have been well, perhaps, if a college for this purpose had been established in England, where the Catholic clergy would have been educated in some degree without the sphere of Irish politics and passions; but such a college was founded in Ireland at Maynooth. It is so clear, that if we undertook to create an institution of this kind we should have done so generously and munificently, that it seems superfluous to waste an argument upon the subject. We had not, however, acted in that large and comprehensive spirit which the occasion demanded; the sum we had dedicated (£9,000 per annum) to the maintenance of an establishment most important to the welfare of so large a portion of our population, was wholly inadequate for its object. Sir Robert Peel now proposed to increase the allowance, and thus to give a proof that the English Government was not indifferent to any class of British subjects, whether within or without the pale of the dominant Church.

It is terrible to find recorded in any page of our modern history that the attempt to provide decorously for the education of the Catholic, was regarded as a grievance by the Protestant; but so it was. Although the principle involved in the Maynooth grant was already conceded,—although neither George III., nor Lord Eldon, nor the Protestants at the Protestant epoch of 1795, had objected to this principle,—it was now assailed as if it had been for the first time propounded, and a bigotry displayed by fanatics, which almost justified agitators. The Premier said, "Abuse me if you will, but let my measure be carried." He was abused, and his measure was carried.

I have said that when he undertook to form a new Conservative party he was obliged to use the old Conservative materials, and that these were the Irish Protestants and the English country gentry. In his endeavour to give to these two bodies a more national character, he had already lost his prestige with the one, and damaged it with the other. Another crisis, however, had yet to arrive, before the career he had entered upon was closed. I approach the repeal of the Corn Laws.

II.

A most rapid change had taken place in public opinion within but a few years about the laws concerning corn. From the earliest period of my public life I had considered them untenable and dangerous to the class which fancied itself interested in their maintenance. Thus, I voted for their total repeal as early as 1832, but only two persons (Mr. Hume and Mr. Cobbett) voted with me.

Almost every statesman, in fact, up to 1840, had considered, as a matter of course, that home-grown corn was to be protected by a duty on foreign corn. They might differ as to the manner in which that duty should be imposed, as to what should be its amount, but no one doubted that there should be a duty sufficient to procure a remunerative price to the English grower. Mr. Charles Pelham Villiers has the credit of first bringing this subject before the serious attention of politicians. Ere long the Corn Law League was formed, and produced, no doubt, a great effect on the public mind; but this was in consequence of the fact that when the Corn Law League commenced its labours, people's thoughts had been subjected to an influence different from that which had formerly governed them.

Previous to the Reform Bill and the Municipality Bills every body in England looked up: the ambitious young man looked up to the great nobleman for a seat in Parliament; the ambitious townsman to the chief men of his borough for a place in the corporation. Subsequently to these measures, men desirous to elevate their position looked down. The aristocratic tendency of other days had thus become almost suddenly a democratic one. This democratic tendency, which has gone on increasing, had made itself already visible at the period when the Corn Law agitation began. It had been natural until then to consider this subject in relation to the interests of the upper classes; it was now becoming natural to consider it in relation to the interests of the lower classes. The question presented itself in a perfectly different point of view, and politicians found, somewhat to their surprise, that all former arguments had lost their force. It was this change in the spirit of the times which had occasioned within such a very few years a total change in the manner of looking at matters affected by the Legislature. We must, whether we wish to do so or not, breathe the atmosphere that is around us. Directly it was shown them that low wages did not necessarily follow a low price of corn, and that the labourer did not earn more because his living was dearer, the only argument that was still listened to against foreign competition disappeared. Statesman after statesman felt himself gliding into the conviction that all attempts to maintain the existing state of things, because it was thought favourable to the country gentry, was impracticable.

Lord John Russell and other leading members of the Whig party, who had been supporters of a Corn Law, underwent, year by year a modification in their former opinions, and were arriving in 1845 at the determination of abandoning them. Sir Robert Peel had been undergoing precisely the same influences, and was arriving precisely at the same conclusions. The country gentlemen amongst the Whigs had quite as much cause to reproach their leader for an alteration in his views as the country gentlemen of the Tories had a right to reproach theirs. But neither the one statesman nor the other had as yet gone so far as to make common cause with Mr. Villiers and Mr. Cobden. An important and alarming incident hastened the decision of both. That incident was the failure of the potato-crop. Unless some measure was taken for bringing food from foreign countries into England, and especially into Ireland, there was legitimate cause for apprehending a famine. An apprehension of this kind involves no ordinary responsibility. Lord John Russell and Sir Robert Peel felt this almost at the same moment. But whilst the responsibility of the one was far greater than that of the other, his course was far more embarrassed. Lord John did not rely chiefly on those persons who fancied that their income depended on upholding the value of home produce. Sir Robert Peel did. The first might gain office by declaring that the moment was come for putting Protection altogether on one side; the other could only lose it.

Such a consideration might in many cases fairly weigh with a public man. A change of administration, a dislocation of parties, may affect a variety of questions, as well as the one which at the moment may be most prominent. But when the matter which presents itself before you is the death by starvation of hundreds or thousands of your fellow-creatures, and you think, whether rightly or wrongly, that your decision can save or condemn so many existences, is there any one who could counsel you for any reason whatever to sanction wholesale murder by suppressing your convictions? There were persons who did not think famine imminent. To them, of course, the question presented itself in a different point of view. But Sir

Robert Peel seems to have been finally convinced that nothing short of a suspension of the Corn Laws, and the proposal of measures tending to their ultimate abolition, would meet the urgency of the case. He had already lost his confidence in the policy of protecting corn under ordinary circumstances; and now came circumstances which, even if his general opinions had been the same as formerly, would have created an especial reason for putting them on one side.

What was he to do? Some of his colleagues dissented altogether from his views. They did not see the crisis he foresaw so clearly as he did, and therefore were not for meeting it by a temporary suspension of a permanent duty. They did not recognise the necessity for eventually repealing that duty, and therefore were not for proposing measures that would lead to its ultimate abolition. The Premier might have attempted the policy he had in view with the remainder of the ministry, but he wisely resolved on not making such an attempt; and tendering his resignation to her Majesty, and indicating the causes, he stated his readiness to support Lord John Russell if he were willing, and able, to form a Cabinet that would undertake to carry out the views which he believed

Lord John and himself entertained in common. The Whig leader failed in executing the commission with which, after this communication, the Queen intrusted him; and Lord Stanley, now at the head of the Protectionist party, considering it was not in his power to form a Government, Sir Robert Peel had as a matter of duty and necessity to resume his post.

It appears to me that the fact that he had resigned office on changing his policy, and that he did not return to it until every other ministerial combination had failed, rendered his course on this occasion more clear than on the Catholic question. To accuse him under such circumstances of changing his views in order to retain his office is as absurd as unjust. He is not even subject to the charge of retaining power after changing the opinions that he entertained on receiving it. His conduct appears to me to have been dictated by the purest patriotism, and the most complete sacrifice of personal ambition to public motives. Nor was his ability ever more conspicuous than during the ordeal he had now to undergo.

It is not, however, my intention to follow him through the Parliamentary contest in which he was soon engaged, and out of which he came triumphant, though not without, for the second time in his life, having been submitted to the severest obloquy, and having exposed his friends, which must have been his most painful trial, to accusations as bitter as those which he had himself to support.

The event which he must have anticipated was now at hand.

We know that, according to Mahomedan superstition a man walks through life with his good and his bad angel by his side. Sir Robert Peel had at this moment his good and his bad angel accompanying his political fortunes with equal pace.

"During the progress of the Corn Law Bill," he says in his Memoirs, "through the two Houses of Parliament, another bill, entitled a Bill for the Protection of Life in Ireland, which at an early period of the Session had received the assent of the House of Lords, was brought under discussion in the House of Commons, and encountered every species of opposition."

* * * * * *

On the 21st of January, 1846, the two bills, the Corn Law Repeal Bill, and the Bill for Protection of Life in Ireland were in such a position in the two Houses respectively, that there appeared every reason to calculate on the double event,—the passing of the first bill unmutilated by the House of Lords, and the rejection of the second by the House of Commons. These two bills were indeed his guardian and destroying angels. The one crowned him with imperishable fame—the other ejected him for the last time from power.

On the 19th of May, 1846, the Corn Law Repeal Bill was carried by a majority of 98. On the 25th of June, by a concerted union between the Protectionists and Whig parties, the Irish Life Protection Bill was rejected by a majority of 75, and the Premier retired, the shouts of congratulation at his victory mingling with the condolence at his defeat. One farther triumph, however, yet remained to him, that of supporting the Whig Government, when, but a short time afterwards, it deemed itself obliged to bring forward a bill almost similar to the one which when proposed by an opposite party it had denounced. The most triumphant portion of Sir Robert Peel's political career was indeed that which followed his exclusion from official life. I know of no statesman who ever occupied so proud a position as that in which a greater commoner than even the first William Pitt stood from 1846 to July, 1850, when an unhappy accident filled with patriotic sorrow, every heart in England. Above all parties, himself a party,—he had trained his own mind into a disinterested sympathy with the intelligence of his country. He never during this period gave a vote to court democratic influence or to win aristocratic favour. Conscientiously and firmly attached to the religion of the state, he flattered none of its prejudices, and repudiated boldly its exclusive pretensions; and his speech on the Jewish Disabilities Bill, considering that it was delivered towards the close of a career which had begun under the intolerant patronage of Lord Eldon, is perhaps the most notable and the most instructive that he ever delivered, as marking the progress of opinion during forty years in the history of England.

III.

If it could be said of any man, indeed, it could be said of this statesman, that time in its progress turned him inside out. But the process was a gradual one, and it was only when you put the Peel of 1810 by the side of the Peel of 1850, that the totality of the change appears distinct. And yet, though the end of Sir Robert Peel's career was at such variance with the commencement, there is a certain consistency that may be traced throughout it. Formed on those official habits which incline a minister to postpone or oppose the consideration of all questions which cannot be successfully dealt with, he never exposed a theory until it could be realized, nor brought forward a measure which he did not think he could carry. At the same time his tendencies were liberal whenever the object brought under his consideration became practical. It must also be said that in the matter on which these tendencies came most strikingly into view his objects were Conservative.

He was converted with respect to the Catholic question, and was converted to Liberal views, but when he professed this conversion, it was to save the country from civil war. He was converted with respect to the Corn Law, and was converted to Liberal convictions; but when he professed this conversion, it was to save the country from famine.

Those who have asserted that his natural bent was towards a change in established institutions and ancient customs, were, I think, decidedy wrong. His natural disposition was rather to maintain what he found existing, but he sacrificed old things without scruple when he considered them decidedly incompatible with new ideas. He had not that order of mind which creates and forces its creations on the minds of others. His mind was, on the contrary, a recipient which opened gradually to growing opinions, and became another mind as these opinions got by degrees possession of it. His changes were thus more sudden in appearance than in reality, because they always went on for a certain time, silently, and to a certain degree unconsciously to himself as well as to the world before they were fully felt; nor were they ever publicly announced till, having passed through a stage of doubt, they arrived at the stage of conviction. His convictions, moreover, were generally simultaneous with those of the public, when the public formed its convictions gradually. But any sudden and unexpected leap of opinion, as in the case of the Whig Reform Bill of 1832, took him unprepared. His manner in personal intercourse, however intimate your relations might be, was nearly always formal, though not cold; but in correspondence he was easy, natural, and remarkable for the simplicity and frankness of his letters.

I speak at least from the result of my own experience. In all matters of home policy he was thoroughly master of every subject that could interest an English statesman. In foreign matters he had general notions, but not much knowledge of particulars, nor any special plan or theory of policy; but a high idea of the power of England and the expediency of maintaining her dignity and prestige.

In the early part of his life I have no doubt that ambition, and the personal motives of ambition, had a certain influence over his actions. At a later period, in his last administration, and after quitting office, I believe he had no personal view that separated him in the slightest degree from an entire and disinterested devotion to the interests of his country. He was a scholar in the highest sense of the term; nor did the attention he could give to the dryest details of business damp his sympathy for the elegancies of literature, or his appreciation of what was beautiful, whether in painting or sculpture. He had no hatred—no inveterate prejudices against persons or things. His domestic virtues are too well known to make it necessary to allude to them.

In short, without pretending to raise him above the defects and littlenesses of human nature, I do not know where to point to any one who united such talents for public business with such qualities in private life.

IV.

A comparison which suggests itself naturally to those who study the history of their times, is one between the practical statesman, the sketch of whose career I am concluding, and his more brilliant contemporary, of whom I have previously spoken. Though for a long period rivals, they both entered political life under the Tory banner, and gained their reputation by adopting Whig principles. In canvassing their separate merits, it is just to say that Sir Robert Peel's great acts were the development of Mr. Canning's principles. The former hatched the latter's ideas, and for one triumph especially, which Sir Robert tardily but nobly achieved, the Catholics of the British empire must feel even more grateful to their early champion than to their subsequent benefactor.

Sir Robert Peel had the talents for giving a prosperous issue to a popular cause, Mr. Canning the genius that makes a cause popular. The one had the courage to advocate an opinion before it was ripe for realisation. The other, the fortitude when the advantage and the possibility of a measure became apparent, to make unhesitatingly every personal sacrifice for the public welfare. If we praise the one for his prescience as a statesman, we bend with admiration before the other as a patriot.

The brilliant talents, the genial and generous spirit of Mr. Canning procured him partizans who served him with their heart, and animating his country by a sympathy with his spirit, inspired a sort of affectionate interest in his fortunes. The calm and steady prudence, the sober and moderate language, the punctilious devotion to business, the constant attention to practical and useful improvements, the comprehensive acquirements, the gradual abandonment of early prejudices, won by degrees for Sir Robert Peel a sort of judicial pre-eminence which made men obey his decisions who were displeased with his manners, and who even differed from his opinions. Thus was he finally elevated to a height in the general esteem which was the more remarkable from its being gained by qualities which neither charmed individuals nor dazzled the public.

Each left a school. In the one we may learn how to sustain our renown and our power abroad; in the other how to advance our prosperity at home. Both were the citizens of a free state, but if I might venture to distinguish the peculiarities of these two illustrious Englishmen by a reference to classical examples, I would say that the one resembled a Greek in the most glorious times of Athens, the other reminded you of a Roman in the noblest epoch of the city of Romulus.

THE END.

LONDON: PRINTED BY WILLIAM CLOWES AND SONS, STAMFORD STREET
AND CHARING CROSS.

www.ingramcontent.com/pod-product-compliance
Lightning Source LLC
Chambersburg PA
CBHW030346170426
43202CB00010B/1262